TRAINING THE
WORKING
SPANIEL

TRAINING THE WORKING SPANIEL

Janet Menzies

Quiller

For Nancarrow Dutch,
the best worst Cocker Spaniel ever

First published in the UK in 2010
by Quiller, an imprint of Quiller Publishing Ltd

Reprinted 2012, 2014

British Library Cataloguing-in-Publication Data
    A catalogue record for this book
    is available from the British Library

ISBN 978 1 84689 070 3

Printed in China

Quiller
An imprint of Quiller Publishing Ltd
Wykey House, Wykey, Shrewsbury, SY4 1JA
Tel: 01939 261616 Fax: 01939 261606
E-mail: info@quillerbooks.com
Website: www.countrybooksdirect.com

CONTENTS

ACKNOWLEDGEMENTS

Spaniel people are without doubt the most sporting and helpful bunch of men and women I have come across in any sphere of life. Training and competing our spaniels together is always tremendous fun, even if things don't go perfectly on an individual basis. So, in no particular order, and not exclusively, here are the people who made this book possible.

Exmoor picker-up Jan Brown got me into gundogs. Professional spaniel and sniffer-dog trainer Eric Burchell suggested I try field trialling. Professional spaniel trainer Jonathan Bailey (patiently supported by his wife Catherine) has handled several of my Cockers with great success. Spaniel professional Ian Openshaw and his wife Wendy have generously given me excellent advice. Simon Tyers and Will Clulee have both provided great Cocker stud dogs, siring delightful and successful pups for the Gournaycourt line. Lady Pat Rhodes gave me a wonderful welcome to the Cocker Club. Ian Flint persuaded me not to sell a future champion. Howard and Jennifer Day have put up with cast-off pups as well as shooting over the better ones for me. John Cook has given me unfailing help, as he does across the spaniel board, even including Clumbers. My gamekeeper, Ian Applin, has had trialling rules inflicted on him. Terry Frost picked me the very best of his Springer pups. All the secretaries of the different trialling clubs work non-stop to make our sport run smoothly. Regular fellow trials competitors/judges include Dave Lisset, Andrew and Fiona Robinson, Mike Wills, Peter Jones, Roy Ellershaw, Dai Ormond, Mark Colclough, Mark Whitehouse, John Dixon, Bob Crowther, Eddy Scott and the entire gang – you

OPPOSITE: *Jon Bailey with the author's FTCh Gournaycourt Morag*

probably don't realise how much I am always learning from you all! I'm pleased to say that this book isn't just one person's idea of how to train your spaniel, but includes all the excellent advice I have taken on board over the years.

The author is congratulated by Her Majesty The Queen after the 2008 Cocker Spaniel Championship at Sandringham (CHARLES SAINSBURY-PLAICE)

INTRODUCTION: MEET THE GUINEA-PUPS

My most memorable spaniel training lesson was taught me in the middle of a Scottish heather moor by Ian Openshaw, the most consistently successful professional spaniel handler of recent years. I was failing to direct Nancarrow Dutch onto a retrieve when Ian came over to me. 'Hold on a minute, Jan,' he said, 'Close your eyes and turn round.' Expecting some miracle of gundog handling, I obediently did so. 'Now tell me which way I'm pointing,' said Ian, adding: 'You can open your eyes if you want.' I opened my eyes and gazed out across the glorious purple haze of late August heather stretching away above Amulree. But I was none the wiser about where Ian was pointing.

I was forced to admit: 'I have no idea which way you're pointing, Ian.'

'So why is that?'

'Because I'm not actually looking at you.'

'OK, now you can turn round.'

Which I did, and immediately saw Ian's hand signal. The point was well made. I had been giving Dutch hand signals when he wasn't looking at me. No wonder he didn't obey them – he hadn't even seen them! If you want to give your spaniel direction onto a retrieve, you must first have him sat up and looking at you so that he can see what you are doing. Duh …

I don't feel embarrassed about telling this shaming tale of handler incompetence, because I see this same fault almost every time I go out shooting. Even if I was the only person who had ever made that mistake, I would still tell the story, because it demonstrates two fundamental principles of gundog training which I hope will inform this whole book. The most obvious of course, is that common sense is just as important when training a dog as in every other area of life. You may forget your slip-lead or even your whistle when you take your dog out, but the one thing you mustn't leave behind is your brain.

Ian's lesson also taught me that a lifetime of reading books (I have an MA in English Literature from Cambridge University, as well as an MA in Creative Writing) is not always helpful when the chips are down out there in the field. Therefore I have tried to make this book as close to the real thing as possible. I'm going to be telling it like it is when it comes to training your spaniel. I hope this will be especially useful for those training their first spaniel, but since every dog is different, it will be relevant for all of us.

So now let's meet the 'guinea-pups'. At the time of writing, I am training three young spaniels. As I write this book I am going to be putting all the theory I talk about into practice with the guinea-pups, and I will honestly report exactly how well (or otherwise) it all turns out.

Guinea-pup number one is an English Springer Spaniel, Frostfields Ricky, aged nearly eight months. Ricky was bred by Terry Frost out of his FTCh bitch Gowerhey Mystique, by FTCh Maesyronen Markettrader, who recently gained a diploma of merit at the English Springer Spaniel Championship. The other two guinea-pups are Cocker Spaniels: Gournaycourt Ginger and Gournaycourt Pepper, a brother and sister, four months old, bred by me. They are the third generation of Gournaycourt Cockers. Their grandmother, FTCh Abbeygale May, is now eleven but still comes out shooting with undiminished charisma. Her daughter, the pups' mum, is FTCh Gournaycourt Morag, third placed at the 2008 Cocker Spaniel Championship, handled for me by Jon Bailey. Their father is Will Clulee's FTCh Argyll Warrior.

These three youngsters are all field trial-bred through and through, with a very high percentage of champions and championship-winners going back across five generations and more in their family trees. Already, they are proving the argument for holding field trials and for breeding from successful trialling dogs. All three have learnt voice, whistle and hand commands more or less at the first time of asking, and they all have soft, willing and affectionate temperaments. When Simon Tyers won the 2007 Cocker Spaniel Championship with FTCh Timsgarry Barlow (another son of FTCh Argyll Warrior), only nineteen months old at the time, he modestly told onlookers that the dog had been 'almost self-training'. But don't run away with the idea that these well-bred dogs don't need training! Dogs like Simon's are quick learners and naturally talented, but they

OPPOSITE: *The author sends FTCh Gournaycourt Morag on a retrieve while the next generation watches*

still need to learn the basics, and the better they get, the more important it is to maintain discipline.

I can already tell this is going to be vital with Gournaycourt Ginger. He is exceptionally bold, with an instinctive drive and will to win. He is a natural retriever, having picked up and carried any object pretty much as soon as he could walk and hold his head up. I have been taking him out on little 'mock hunting' trips round our fields and I can see that he has a naturally good hunting style. His early lessons in basic commands and hand signals have also gone very well. All this fills me with anxiety, because I can foresee trouble to come! Professional spaniel trainer Jon Bailey warns: 'It's the good ones with plenty of drive that end up tipping over the edge.' He's right. As with a bright child at school who finds all the lessons easy; boredom, cheekiness and naughtiness can soon set in. So I'm preparing myself for a few confrontations when Ginger really finds his paws in a couple of months time.

You should take time to think about your own puppy in this way. Is he a bit of a cheeky chappy – an Artful Dodger of a pup? Or is he more like Oliver Twist, trusting and obedient? Where Ginger has definite Dodger tendencies, his sister, Pepper, is the Oliver type. Very sweet-natured, she is also a little timid, which could hold her back when training becomes more demanding. As you start training your own pup, remember your assessment of him and adapt your training style accordingly. Keep reassessing him. Puppies' temperaments can change a lot as they mature. Knowing your pup will help you plan how to train him. If you have a Dodger type you can be a little bit tougher and push a bit harder. You also know you have to keep discipline in mind much more than you do with an Oliver. With the softer, Oliver-type, you may have to be a bit more patient and progress slowly. It doesn't matter in the long run. Those lessons learnt slowly often stick better than the ones picked up quickly.

The Springer pup, Ricky, is a good example of a dog learning fast, but not necessarily thoroughly. He is very willing and bonded to me, so picks up new lessons quickly. However he isn't as mentally mature as the Cockers and can be thoroughly goofy at times. Some dogs tend to learn in fits and starts, and your job as a trainer is to even out those peaks and troughs. With Ricky I must make sure I don't try to over-stretch him on an off day, or bore him on a good day. It's a difficult task, but as long as you are tuned-in to your dog, it's achievable.

As you get ready to meet your own new pup and start those early socialisation lessons, try to get your mind-set sorted out. You are going to be the central figure in your dog's life – even more than you are with your children. For training and later, in working, you will expect your dog's undivided attention whenever you ask for it. Equally though, you must be prepared to commit your full concentration to your dog when you are training and working together. If your dog looks to you, and you are looking away, don't be surprised when he finds something else to look at. By far the biggest problem-causer for amateur handlers is that they don't take enough interest in their dogs.

You also need to have a plan and goals right from the outset – and that's where this book will be a big help to you. Read it all the way through to the end before you set off training. That way you will have some idea of the road ahead, where you are going, and how you might get there, rather like a sat-nav for gundog work. Particularly if this is the first dog you are training, it is important to know what you are aiming at as the finished result. When I began training my first Cocker I had no idea quite how close and tight their quartering pattern should be when hunting. My main experience of gundogs was Labradors goofing about retrieving stuff randomly at the end of big pheasant drives. It wasn't until I attended my first spaniel field trial that I realised that precision bird-dogging is not only possible and very effective, but also hugely satisfying and great fun.

Even if you haven't the slightest intention of your spaniel ever setting paw on a field trial, do try to visit one or two as a spectator. Despite the rise in popularity of hunt/point/retrieve breeds, no one seriously contests the view that the spaniel is the most complete all-round gundog and you need to be able to see how much they can do in order to believe it! When you have trained your spaniel to perfection (and you will) he will quarter in front of you to hunt up game well within gunshot range. When he has found a bird he will flush it and then sit absolutely still while you shoot, called dropping to flush. If you decide not to shoot the bird or it doesn't flush for some reason, he will leave it on command and continue to hunt on. If you decide to retrieve the game (perhaps a previously wounded bird) he will retrieve it on command. If you happen to shoot a rabbit or bird which he has not flushed, he will drop to the sound of your shot. When you shoot game (whether he has flushed it or not) he will mark its fall as far as possible. Your spaniel will not go out to retrieve the fallen game unless you command him (yes, you did read that right, and yes, what you see every day on most shoots is a huge fault). When you do send him, he will go swiftly to the marked fall and bring the game directly back to you without stopping to chase other birds or pick up other falling game (or passing go and collecting £200 for that matter). If the fall has not been marked – a blind retrieve – you can stop him wherever he is and give him hand, voice and whistle signals until the bird is found. Very often your spaniel won't need much help from you, instead using his splendid nose to follow the blood scent of wounded game that has made its best way to the nearest ditch.

A moderately good spaniel can do all this, and loves doing it – and what's more, *will* do it if given a reasonably thorough training. A brilliant spaniel can do the whole thing with one paw tied behind its back, plus achieving more than you ever thought possible. My first champion, Kelmscott Whizz (Lynn) had the great knack of getting the far side of game so that she could flush it back towards you – a far easier shot than the normal going-away. It made every day a mini-driven one. When trialling, it had the added advantage that even the most inattentive of hip-flask swigging Guns couldn't fail to kill the bird, making for lots of nice, straightforward retrieves and A-grades in the judges' notebooks. My second, rather quirkier champion, Abbeygale May (Tippy) would constantly surprise us with antics that only made sense once her full game plan had played out. On one trial she began digging frantically under a log. She then ran round to the other side of the log and started digging there too, before coming back round again. We waited for her to be ejected from the trial, but sure enough there was a rabbit sitting deep under the log, and sure enough, it bolted straight through Tippy's previously prepared tunnel, directly into the line of shot of the waiting Gun. It was like something out of Blue Peter (without the cardboard loo roll), and of course she won the trial.

Such moments are why we bother to train our dogs properly, and why shooting over a well-trained spaniel is such a lasting joy. One of my greatest shooting memories of all time is of the first spaniel I attempted to train, dear old mad-dog Dutch. By dint of not taking mounds of very good advice, I made rather a poor job of training Dutch, but every dog has his day, and Dutch's came walking-up grouse at Castle Grant in Strathspey. The pointers had been defeated by an unpredictable back wind and we had resorted to spaniels. As we worked our way back to the vehicles, the better spaniels were running out of steam. Dutch's turn came up. He quartered busily through the heather and then half-pointed before flushing a singleton cock bird right in front of us. Bless him, he dropped instantly, while I killed the bird with a single shot (handlers can have their day too). He then waited while I broke my gun and sent him for the retrieve, which he returned to me in a trice. Larks sang, the heather smelt of honey, picnic lunch was waiting. The only function of the rest of our shooting party was to applaud.

You too will have days like this with your first spaniel, so no wonder you are itching to get started. Naturally the first question everybody asks is: 'How old should my puppy be before I start training him?' Professional gundog trainers

The author with foundation bitches FTCh Gournaycourt Morag (left) and her mother FTCh Abbeygale May, aged eleven

are usually irritatingly hard to pin down about this, saying things like: 'as soon as it is ready'. I have gradually come to the conclusion that what they really mean is both 'Now', and 'Never'. The 'now' is the bonding, socialising and communicating with your pup which starts from the moment you first see him. Communicating with your pup is at the heart of all your future training success, so in a sense you have already started training your pup. If you get these very early moments right, the more formal training process will be much easier. Many professionals training a lot of youngsters for themselves and clients are aware that they haven't enough time to give each pup the individual early attention it needs and so they find loving family homes to do the doting for the first few months of the puppy's life. This is one area where you as an amateur with just one or two dogs are at a distinct advantage over the professional – so don't waste it!

The 'Never' aspect of training a pup is that as far as possible it should never have the feeling that it is being Trained with a capital T. All that early bonding will evolve naturally into a desire to please you, so that training becomes merely a matter of finding ways to explain to your dog what it is that you want him to do. As soon as you have successfully communicated with each other, so that he understands what you want, he will do it. As you train your youngster, you will be amazed to discover what a team you both are. You are on the same side and have the same objectives. He wants to hunt, flush and retrieve. You want him to hunt, flush and retrieve. It really is as simple as that. The main difference of opinion you are likely to encounter is an occasional disagreement about the amount of control needed to perform the operation. This is called 'steadiness' and is probably the most difficult concept to get across to an enthusiastic young spaniel. But bear in mind all the time, that most of the problems you are likely to come across in the next eighteen months of training will be down to failure of communication at heart. So whenever things are getting sticky, think of that first. How can I communicate better to this idiot dog? Why is he not getting it today? There will be lots of different answers to this, which we will explore in the 'trouble shooting' section of each chapter.

The very first thing you need to communicate to your pup, and ultimately the only really vital thing, is the difference between right and wrong. It is fundamental, not just to the trained gundog, but to every dog which is living in domestic surroundings. And yet – and please excuse me while I fume – how often do we see a dog being walked in the park that hasn't got the faintest idea of right and wrong? How often does the owner mumble: 'Oh he's only playing' as some twenty kilogram Golden Retriever bowls up in a dominant way to a two-year-old toddler and proceeds to put its paws up on the unfortunate child's shoulders? In dog language large physical displays like this are assertions of dominance and can be a prelude to aggression. It has as much to do with play as Mike Tyson's ear-biting has to do with boxing. A dog which is playing will roll over on its back, or drop a shoulder, or play-bow – quite the opposite of jumping up. Whether we are gundog trainers or park-walkers, in our hearts we all know when a dog is doing wrong. It is our responsibility on every level to correct a dog that is doing wrong.

If you start when the pup is still young, impressionable and dependent, teaching right from wrong is easy. You just praise the pup when he is doing right and tell him off when he is doing wrong. It is that simple. Nor does it need to be a big thing – just a nice warm tone of voice for a good dog, and a sharp 'ach, ach' for a bad dog – nothing more is needed. But you must do it consistently. Wrong doesn't suddenly become right just because it is a sunny day. Right doesn't turn into wrong if you are having a row with your girlfriend. The Zen of dog training is absolute – this is one set of modern morals which is inflexible!

Your own personality will help a lot with this. If you are a calm, assertive kind of person with a good idea of who you are and where you are going in life, you will find dogs are pretty biddable with you. Sadly, if you wouldn't say boo to a goose, you are going to find it equally hard to say 'stop that' to a dog – and many dogs will tease you for it. But the good news is that dogs are a lot easier to deal with than humans. The confidence gained from creating a fantastic bond with your dog is often a great booster in other areas of your life. Personally, I am well known for my bossy and forthright temperament, developed during my former life as a Fleet Street newspaper executive with a kennel-full of young writers to be steadied, and which works just as well with boisterous young spaniels.

So far I haven't had to be bossy with either Ginger or Pepper. Even when they were only three months old they always got plenty of praise for rushing round retrieving rolled-up socks. Equally they got a tiny, puppy-size telling off for nibbling human toes. As they get older a sharp cough is all it takes to remind them that they are doing the wrong thing – but they much prefer doing the right thing because then they get their tummies tickled. Ricky is beginning to reach the adolescent stage of pushing the boundaries a bit – mainly just to see what happens. Because he learnt right stuff from wrong stuff early on, he does know when he is doing the wrong thing. So it doesn't come really come as a surprise to him when the result is a verbal ticking off and a cross boss. It is probably a security thing. As he becomes more independent, he is checking that the old puppy rules are still there like always. If I hadn't taught him good and bad right at the beginning, this stage would now be much more difficult and confusing for him.

That's enough about my pups; let's get on with training yours. At the end of the book there is a glossary of all the commands and terms you will need to know (revision for those who already use them).

Part One: Training your Spaniel from Puppy to Eighteen Months

1.
FIRST PRINCIPLES

So far I have yet to meet anyone (including myself) with the presence of mind to buy a gundog training book *before* buying a puppy, so this first chapter assumes that you are now excitedly preparing to go and collect your eight-week-old puppy from the breeder. A later chapter, when we are all calmer, will give some hints on buying or breeding the next puppy. But there are a few preparations you need to make now, before you collect the pup. The most important thing at this point is to decide where the puppy will live, both in its early months and throughout its life. Whether your spaniel lives in the house or in a kennel in the long term says a lot about how serious you are as a gundog handler – as well as quite a bit about how muddy your spaniel is!

Labrador owners tend to be able to get away with their dogs living in the kitchen or entrance hall, since these lugubrious peg-sitters have a predisposition to stay where they are told (especially if there is telly to watch or pizza to be eaten). Whereas no spaniel worth its salt is going to rest until it has hunted up every square inch of your house at least twice. One of our Cocker pups escaped into the guest suite, where it rapidly flushed a stale ham and cheese sandwich from the waste paper basket. I knew it was going to be good (the dog, not the sandwich) because it brought the sandwich back to me rather than eating it.

I find that once they are working, my spaniels can't really relax in the house. If I'm there they expect full-on hunting fun and don't like me concentrating on stirring the hollandaise sauce rather than on them. But the pups are all born in the kitchen and then weaned into an indoor pen in the back corridor before they eventually become too much of a handful and go out to their proper kennel at about four months old (a great relief for us all!). If you are going to keep your dog in the house permanently, then definitely invest in a large indoor dog pen which can be the dog's private quarters throughout its life. The pen needs to be big enough for the full-grown dog to curl up in and also stand upright. Some very well-known top shots and lords of the land have their dogs in their houses and even on their beds, but they are fairly relaxed about both the state of their counterpanes and the behaviour of their dogs. I don't think you will ever quite have the right working relationship with a dog that lives in the house, but it is a matter of personal preference. What you certainly must not do is let the dog up on furniture or have it in the same room where you are eating or sleeping. This throws the pecking order right out, and you will find it very hard to maintain your dog's respect for you.

Along with the indoor pen you need to buy some 'vet bed' and two or three stainless steel feeding bowls, as well as saving up loads of newspapers. Also buy a puppy-size dog collar and clip-on lead. Find out what your breeder is feeding the pup and buy a few packs of it. I also like to have some tins of rice pudding handy, as it's a great food to aid dietary transitions, upset stomachs etc. It is not essential to buy training equipment now, but it's hard to hold back. So here are the basics:

- **3 x 210 ½ whistles on lanyards.** Keep one of these whistles permanently in the glove compartment of your shooting vehicle, where it will regularly save your life when you forget your whistle. The other two can live in the kitchen, gunroom, wherever.
- **3 x brightly coloured, cheap slip-leads.** Keep one in the kennel, one in the vehicle and one in your dog training bag. Ideally buy more than three. You can lose that number in a week (hence cheapness and bright colour).
- **Some old tennis balls.**
- **Some old pairs of socks rolled up into balls.** These are great for young pups. They can be thrown or rolled and they are light to carry and easy for a puppy's small mouth. They can easily be stuffed into the pocket when going out for some spur-of-the-moment training. For some reason puppies seem to carry them very well and gently without gripping. Also they double as gloves if you have to remove something truly disgusting from your puppy's mouth.
- **A canvas dummy.** A lot of trainers are using 'Kong' training aids instead of dummies now. The 'AirKONG' retrieving trainer is made from tennis ball felt, in the shape of a narrow version of a traditional dummy. It has a length of rope attached to make it easier to throw. Look at one on their website, or email for details of your nearest

stockist (See Appendix III). Traditional canvas dummies are made by Turner Richards; you can buy a selection via their website (See Appendix III).

- **A game bag or similar to carry all the above.**
- **A mountaineer's carabineer.** Fitted round the shoulder strap of your game bag, this surprisingly comes in very useful for attaching stuff to (leads, dummies, key rings etc) and also marks you out as a serious spaniel trainer.
- **Waterproof/thorn proof canvas leggings or over trousers.** If you do not have these already they are an absolute must when working or training spaniels. The Cocker hasn't been born that doesn't spend most of its life climbing you, and Springers are no saints either.
- **A 'throw-down' gun.** You won't be shooting over your pup for a long time, but when you do, leave the family's finest Purdeys in the gun cabinet. Instead buy or borrow a cheap basic 20 or 28 bore that you won't mind chucking on the ground if you have to go and extract your dog from trouble in a hurry. If it has swivels for a sling even better. A small calibre is less noisy for a young dog, and lighter to carry when walking all day.
- **Do not buy a starting pistol or dummy launcher.** There is a place for both these items in training, and you may well use them as your dog advances. But they do need a bit of experience to work correctly and they aren't vital. It is best to use them with help from a friend to fire the starting pistol or launcher. An alternative is to book a couple of lessons with a professional for that stage in the dog's training.

Before you set out to collect your puppy, remember to puppy-proof the car. Hopefully you own a 4x4 or hatchback which will take a decent-size travelling dog pen. These are made by Lintran (See Appendix III). You can buy them over the internet, and often you can pick up second-hand ones on e-bay and elsewhere. They last a lifetime. Mine is twenty years old and has been driven over occasionally but is still absolutely fine. Travelling with the pup or grown dog in the passenger foot-well or back seat is borderline illegal and not advisable. It is uncomfortable for the dog being cramped and thrown around and much more likely to cause travel sickness. When the dog is muddy it is a disaster. Much better for the dog to have his own personal travelling space where he can settle down, especially on long journeys. Don't be tempted to get a rail-type dog guard. A couple who didn't head this warning turned up to collect two Cocker pups from us with a cheap'n'cheerful dog guard fitted in the hatch-back. They placed the two little cutey pups in the back and walked round to the front of the car to get in, where they found the pups sitting waiting for them, one on the driver's seat and one on the passenger's. That's how quickly and easily a ten-week-old spaniel can find its way through a dog guard. Line the travelling pen with newspaper and put a sheet of 'vet bed' on top. You can also put in a non-spill bowl of water. For this first ever journey it's likely your puppy will actually travel sitting on a towel on your lap for at least most of the way home, but you may as well get into good habits from the start.

Many breeders allow potential buyers to come and look at the pups about a fortnight before they are ready to go to their new homes. At this point buyers can see the mother, read her pedigree and hopefully admire her 'ego-wall' of field trialling awards, before choosing a pup and paying a small deposit. I prefer this, as it allows you all to build a relationship and avoids disappointments. But when FTCh Gournaycourt Morag managed to produce four little replicas recently, I have to say all were spoken for by word of mouth and people didn't feel the need to see them before carrying them triumphantly off. This is often the way if potentially top class pups enter the world. So if your top field trialling breeder is offering you the chance to buy such a pup, don't be too put off if he would rather you didn't turn up until the pup is eight to ten weeks old and ready to leave. If you have any doubts, get the number of someone else who is also having one of the pups and chat to them. Or the breeder may text you a photo (though a lot of them are rather techno-phobic!).

When you collect the pup, however, there are certain things the breeder must provide you with and you really should insist on these. You will need the Kennel Club's registration certificate with the pup's name and breeding and KC registration number. It will also have a section which you must fill in and send off to the Kennel Club to register the change of ownership. The breeder will sign and date his section when you pay for the pup. Don't let him forget to do this. You should also receive a docking certificate signed and dated by the vet who docked your pup's tail. Check that the details on this certificate match up with those on the Kennel Club documentation. You will also notice that you are legally obliged by the Animal Welfare Act 2006 to have your pup identi-chipped when he is about three months old, so that he can be matched up with his paperwork. Many responsible breeders will remind you about this when they hand you the paperwork. Some spaniel pups may not have had their tails docked, but really if your dog is going to work properly it will need to have had the thin, brittle tip of its tail removed in order to avoid future injury.

Handlers form a strong bond with their dogs (CHARLES SAINSBURY-PLAICE)

In Scotland it is currently illegal to dock any puppy's tail, so if yours was bred in Scotland it is unlikely to be docked. If it is docked, thank your lucky stars and don't enquire too much about it. In England and Wales I would advise caution if the paperwork isn't around, or if the breeder tries to fob you off when you ask about it. Oddly enough, although perceived as an irritation, the Animal Welfare Act is actually helping owners of working spaniels. Theft of working gundogs is on the increase, but as more and more gundogs are readily identifiable, and buyers begin to demand paperwork, gundog theft is gradually becoming less profitable. As buyers, breeders and owners we all need to be responsible about this – it is in our best interests after all. For more on how to protect your puppy against theft, and prevent it generally, have a look at the Dog Theft Action website (See Appedix III).

The other important thing to remember is the pup's vaccinations. My vet likes to give the first injection at around ten weeks old, followed by a booster two weeks later. Some breeders take this on themselves, in which case the pup's price will reflect the cost, but usually you will be expected to organise the jabs once you get the pup home. Be aware that the pup has little immunity until after the vaccinations have 'taken' by about fourteen weeks old. Up until that time you need to keep the pup out of contact with other dogs and places which see heavy dog use. I keep my pups just in the garden until I am sure their immunity is fully developed. Most breeders will hand over a 'puppy pack' including the paperwork, care and training instructions, useful phone numbers etc; a sample of the puppy's food; sometimes a blanket or any small toy he has been using; and of course – the puppy itself!

A ragger is all the training equipment you need to start with...

...a tennis ball will do for retrieving...

...or even a cuddly toy (NICK RIDLEY)

When you get home establish the pup with a small toy (rag-type not squeaky) in his indoor pen on thick layers of newspaper and with a small bowl shallowly filled with water. Then I'm afraid the best thing you can possibly do is leave him alone for a couple of hours to rest and relax. If this is your first spaniel, we now come to the issue of your family and the dog – because this is almost certainly going to be the crucial moment when the whole family want to play and cuddle the new pup and you now have to be the most unpopular person in the house by setting the tone for your pup's future. If this puppy is intended to be mainly a family pet with a bit of gundog work thrown in when you happen to be invited out shooting or beating, then we can all relax and forget about respect, discipline and training. But since you bought a book called *Training the Working Spaniel*, I sense you are really quite serious about having a good gundog by your side in a year or so. That means there have to be rules.

Rule one: decide who in the house is going to be the dog's trainer and main 'primary' handler. You are the one reading the book, so that means you. You are in charge of the dog, you are responsible for his welfare and training, and what you say about the dog is what happens with the dog – no arguments. Whatever your role in the family – Mum, Dad, teenage son, grandfather, general hanger-on – doesn't make a difference to that. You may not be the boss of the household, but if you are the dog's primary handler, in that one area, your word should be law. It is a very old saying that a dog can't serve two masters, which I saw comically illustrated on the shooting field. A family had very sensibly decided to get a fully trained Labrador for their first gundog. The new dog made his debut on the first drive, where Mum (being loaded for by eldest daughter) happened to have drawn a low number peg and Dad (accompanied by eldest son) was shooting at the other end of the line. At the end of the drive the new dog was duly sent out on a retrieve. He reappeared quickly, roughly opposite the centre of the line of Guns, carrying a dead bird. At this point a chorus of 'good boy, bring it in, well done, come here' broke out from opposite ends of the line, as both halves of the family started calling the dog. He stood for a moment, looking right then left like a spectator at Wimbledon, before eventually dropping the bird and trotting off.

Don't shy away from this issue. Dogs need strong leadership, and if you aren't able to assert yourself now, at this very first hurdle, the long-term success of your training the dog is far from guaranteed. There's no need to be bossy or a spoilsport. Of course everybody will have time to play with the puppy. Spaniels (especially Cockers) can soak up as much affection as your entire clan can offer without it impacting their working ability or discipline. FTCh Gournaycourt

Morag (Fudge) won Waggiest Tail and appeared on *Coronation Street* while training to be a gundog and it didn't do her any harm. But now and in the future, there are going to be times when training or resting are more appropriate than play.

Remember too, that as the dog's boss, you also have ultimate responsibility for his wellbeing. If you leave another family member to feed and exercise him all week, you really shouldn't be surprised when the dog continues to be bonded to that family member, despite the fact that you have decided to take him out for half an hour's training today. Unfortunately dogs are very quick to recognise and exploit any power struggles that may be going on within the family. My husband is known as 'non-executive deputy pack leader' which generally means that the dogs consider his commands more in an advisory capacity than anything to be acted on. But at least they aren't getting conflicting input.

This is potentially a problem if you have young children who want to play with the pup when you are not around. Any well-bred spaniel pup starts retrieving as soon as it can toddle and there is nothing more beguiling than watching your little bundle come tottering back to you dragging a slipper twice its size. Once is adorable; twice is charming; three times is a little bit tiring for the puppy; the fourth time is boring; the fifth time it may not retrieve it at all. But getting this message across to your equally adorable six-year-old daughter is difficult.

Children also love giving the pup its little commands. For them it's a sort of remote controlled toy that magically sits when you wave your hand like Daddy did. But child's play is in fact school time for a pup. The trouble comes when your child's capacity to play exceeds the pup's capacity to want to learn. Then you will come home one evening to find a young dog that is thoroughly turned off the idea of answering to his name. Awareness of this potential problem is usually all that is needed to avoid it. If you sense it may become an issue, one solution is to encourage your children to get involved in the pup's early lessons, so that they can see for themselves what is the difference between lessons and relaxation as far as the pup is concerned. But I'm not a child trainer, so ultimately it is up to you how you deal with it if the issue arises. Do deal with it though, or you could easily end up with a sour, non-retrieving young spaniel that doesn't even come when you call. In other words, exactly the kind of dog that you see running wild in the park while his owners claim 'it's only playing'.

If this pup is not just your first spaniel but your first puppy of any sort, a major concern for the family is going to be house-training. There are plenty of guides for first-time dog owners (and house-training isn't peculiar to spaniels!). From my personal successes and failures in this area, I suggest that the indoor pen is your biggest aid to successful house-training. Don't leave a young pup alone for too long, but when you do leave him, shut him into his indoor pen. As soon as you come back, pick him up and take him outside for a little wander until he has thoroughly relieved himself. Likewise, before you are going to leave him, take him out for a quick lavatory break. Do this at regular intervals and you should be fine. One tip – don't rush back indoors as soon as the pup has done his business. Go on playing around for a few minutes, otherwise the pup will associate defecating with the end of play and you will find you are waiting for longer and longer while the pup is holding out as long as possible in order to continue playing – a stand-off that is no fun for humans at 10.30 p.m. on a wet November night!

For the new puppy owner the early concerns are much like those of new parents – learning the routine, the arrival's health, bonding, and bowel movements! Surprisingly there is one other important task in common: the naming of the new family member. Obviously this is a matter of personal taste, but if you want to be serious about having a well-trained dog, try to give him a name you can both respect. The worst behaved chocolate Labs I come across dragging Mums along Sloane Street are all called Cadbury. I suppose you could shorten it to Cad (which they sometimes are), or Bury (and they often should be buried), but Cadbury is not a name of command. You couldn't say it sharply if you needed to. Go for a two-syllable name which can be shortened or lengthened as necessary, and nothing too jokey – it is surprising how un-funny such names become when things go wrong. Lucinda Green, former top three-day-event rider, had a terrier cross which she thought it would be great fun to call Basil. She imagined herself doing a Sybil Fawlty impression, shrieking 'Baaasill!' but when she in fact did end up spending most of her day doing exactly that, the joke wore thin quite quickly.

So now your spaniel has a great name, a secure home environment, a well-ordered routine, and a loving family. This ideal start in life will set you up perfectly for rapid success in the next phase of his life – the first lessons.

TROUBLE SHOOTING

Puppy seems a little weak and isn't growing very fast

Even puppies from top breeders can be very wormy. The worms are passed on by the bitch. With modern wormers you no longer need to wait before worming pups. I worm early on as a matter of course. Keep an eye out for appetite loss, pot-belly, general failure to thrive, which are all signs of worm infestation.

Puppy is whining a lot

Don't be too concerned to begin with. Make sure pup isn't cold, hungry or thirsty. Establish a few familiar things in his pen, especially little rag-toys etc. Then sit it out for a while. If whining is really persistent for more than a couple of days, check for any health causes, e.g. infestation with lice or mites, which might be upsetting the pup. You can also give the breeder a call to see if the behaviour runs in the family.

Puppy is getting very boisterous and difficult already

This is often a symptom of too many family members playing and jazzing-up the pup. Try to stick to good routines. Often a pup that has a lot of ability and drive can seem like a bit of a handful in his early days. Be calm though, the next chapter deals in detail with a pup's first experience of learning right from wrong.

Puppy is chewing everything in sight

Presupposes you left stuff in sight for him to chew. Buy some purpose-made puppy chews (dental chews, rags and rawhide are good) and leave them with the puppy in his pen. Otherwise, if you don't want it chewed, don't leave him alone with whatever it is in tooth-range.

Puppy is very timid

Sometimes happens with a pup from a very large litter or the smallest in the litter, but is very rarely a long-term problem. Although it is counter-instinctive, this pup often benefits from plenty of down-time on his own, which gives him time to familiarise himself with his new surroundings and become more confident in them. Playing a radio in the background often helps. Keep the indoor pen somewhere with a constant gentle trickle of people and sounds, where the pup can see but still feel safe. Don't allow children or strangers unlimited access to pup. Ultimately you can form a wonderful working bond with this softer kind of pup.

Puppy won't house-train

Your fault, not the pup's I'm afraid! Puppies hate soiling their own environment. You must be disciplined in your routines. Feed regularly and have regular, frequent lavatory breaks. Keep the pup in his pen when alone, but never for very long at a time.

2.
EARLY LEARNING

The first question everybody always asks about gundog training is: 'When?!' Professional gundog trainers are quizzed all the time: 'How old should the puppy be before I start training him?' and: 'When can I get going?' or: 'How long should I wait before steadying him?' It is naturally frustrating when trainers answer these questions with all the straightforward forthrightness of an MP explaining his expenses. But the reason they are reluctant to name the day is because there really isn't one. Training your spaniel starts now – and never! Right from the moment he sets paw through the door, your puppy will be learning. Well-bred spaniel pups are usually very bright. They soak up information from human interaction and from their environment. While they are learning so quickly, all you have to do is control the input a little bit. If you get it right at this stage you will drift into formal lessons without either of you really noticing it. The only slightly tedious 'double maths' session that a natural hunting and retrieving spaniel endures is steadiness, and that comes quite a bit later on.

Ginger for example, considers so-called training to be a bit of a doddle. The first time I blew the stop whistle he dropped instantly and sat watching me ready for the next command. He is both intelligent and confident. Although I expected his confidence to lead to naughtiness at some stage, it hasn't yet. I think he finds the commands so easy to learn and perform that there isn't any need to be naughty. But so far I have only been asking him to do his three favourite things – hunting, retrieving, and watching me to see what's coming

---

OPPOSITE: *You should be the most important thing in your dog's life*
(CHARLES SAINSBURY-PLAICE)

next. When we get to steadiness – in other words actual not-hunting and not-retrieving – there could easily be some snags. Ricky, the young Springer, has poor concentration. He learns a new lesson quickly, but tends to forget the previous one in his excitement, so his training needs to be more planned and formal, otherwise we will be going two steps forward and one step backward.

The puppy's very first lesson is the obvious one of knowing his name. When you are cuddling him, tell him his name, and continue to use it frequently. Puppies are extremely responsive to body language. Kneel down or go on hands and knees and say your pup's name. I have never known a pup that didn't come instantly when asked like this. Now add the word 'come' to your pup's name. Within a very short time the pup will learn that: 'Midge, come' means it should return to you. It is the easiest and most obvious thing to teach, as well as being one of the foundations of future training. The puppy comes when called by his name and 'come'. Simple as that. And yet watching novices with their grown dogs (both on the shooting field and at leisure), the single biggest fault I see is dogs not coming when called. What on earth happens between those halcyon days of ten-week-old Midge toddling up as fast as his chubby little legs can go when he hears his name, and two years later when he treats you like a complete stranger? I'm afraid you are what's happened.

If this is your first spaniel (or you have had a training failure), this is likely to be your first lesson as well as the pup's. Puppies tend to learn their early lessons quickly and easily – but they can unlearn them with equal alacrity, especially if a rabbit or the family cat has entered the equation. So consistency is paramount. Once you are certain your puppy knows what to do when he hears you say: 'Midge, come' then he must always do it. If Midge doesn't come when you call, don't call him again. Instead immediately walk up to him and gently drag him towards you while you repeat the command. Next time you ask him to come, you will get a much better reaction. But I don't expect you to have problems at this stage. Very few pups refuse to come unless there is another very tempting distraction, and these temptations usually only appear when the pup is out and about, later in his training. By starting right from day one, while the pup is very dependent, you have the chance to get the lesson really well entrenched before the pup knows anything different.

The next early command is the sit. Just like 'come' it is easy to teach and enforce. Like 'come' it is also a real training fundamental, and yet again, it is a command you see disobeyed all the time on the shooting field. Decide whether you are going to use 'sit' or 'hup' as your command. It is more usual to use the word 'hup' to sit up a spaniel, but use whichever comes naturally to you (and

Ian Openshaw using a clear hand signal for 'hup' (CHARLES SAINSBURY-PLAICE)

your family). Once you have decided, don't change your mind! If you are thinking of sending the pup away to a professional for a couple of months later in his career (and it's often a good idea in order to get use of his facilities), it is worth finding out what commands he uses.

Most trainers recommend using feed time as the best moment to teach sit. In theory you simply wave the food bowl above the dog's head while saying 'hup' or 'sit' and the dog naturally looks up at the bowl, landing on his bum while so doing. Hey presto, you have taught sit. While this works brilliantly with

Labradors – who are both food obsessed and relatively unathletic – it is less sure-fire with spaniels. Cockers especially, are supple enough to look at a raised food bowl without having to sit on their bum, thank you very much. Neither are they that fixated on food. Even so, the feed-time lesson does eventually work with spaniels. Although they are not fixing on the food, they will certainly be fascinated by you and what you are doing. If you stand over the pup with bowl held high, there will be some initial squirming and wriggling, but eventually the pup is likely to sit briefly and look up. Seize this moment to say 'hup' and put the food bowl down in front of the pup.

No matter in how much of a rush you are, you must repeat this process every time you feed the pup, now and always! You will find that the pup learns this command almost as quickly as he learnt 'come' – sometimes in the space of a couple of days. Make sure you keep the ritual going even after the command has been learnt in order to prevent the un-learning syndrome. Once the pup is feeling quite confident and sure of himself and his surroundings you can add another element of this command. First keep the pup waiting a little longer on 'hup' before you put the bowl down. Pups usually tolerate this fairly well, but do watch out for the less hungry kind of pup who might easily give up on the idea of food and wander off. If you sense his attention is beginning to wander, put the bowl down, lesson over.

Once the pup is happy to wait a few seconds in hup before getting his food, add the next stage. Hup the pup, but this time put the bowl down in a position where you are standing between him and the food. Tell the pup 'hup' again and raise your hand as though you were still holding the bowl. A soft, human-centred pup will 'hup' as told just out of surprise and interest in the new thing. A hungrier, less bonded pup will ignore you and go straight for the food. With the pup that hups, keep him in hup for a second, then drop your hand, bend down slightly and say something encouraging like 'take it' as you allow the pup to dash to his food. Make much of him while he is eating. With the pup that didn't hup, because you positioned yourself between him and the bowl, you can physically intervene to grab the pup. Do so. Place him in hup, raise your hand and repeat the command. The pup will get the message quickly and as soon as he has waited a second, let him have the food as with the other pup.

This very simple, very early lesson is much more important than it may seem. It sets the tone for your whole future training of the dog in several ways. First the pup's reaction tells you a lot about the pup. Don't assume the pup that hupped first time is 'good pup' and the one that made a dash for the bowl is 'bad pup'. In fact 'bad pup' is actually showing the greater drive and resolution of the pair. If he then learns quickly to do it how you want, that's even better. It bodes really well for future training. Imagine if that feed bowl were a live rabbit … 'bad pup' effectively has bolted it, as well as learning to stop and wait at your command, despite the temptation to continue eating/chasing. So 'bad pup' has really learnt a genuine lesson: that there are times when you and he want different things, and that is the moment when he must do what you want rather than what he wants.

'Good pup' on the other hand, hasn't really learnt anything much at all, because he wasn't that interested in going for the bowl in the first place. Only when the pup wants to do something a different way from how you want is he really learning about your future relationship. Pepper is a good example of this. She doesn't like being watched eating, and so would wait for her food in any case. With her I have had to find a slightly different way of teaching 'hup'. From the moment she could walk she has always been obsessed with retrieving and carrying any object (regardless of size). So instead of using a feed bowl for this exercise, I have substituted a small raggy toy. I hold this above her head and continue with the lesson just as described with the feed bowl, giving her the toy (never throw, that would be a different lesson), just as I do the feed bowl.

The feed bowl is by far the commonest technique for teaching pups to sit, but I think it should come with a slight warning. Those who usually train large dog breeds (Labradors etc) depend on the voracious appetite of those breeds. But smaller working dogs, especially Cockers, are often picky eaters and even future champions can be very neurotic with food. With this kind of pup I concentrate on getting them to eat immediately and quickly rather than messing around at feed times. Often these pups are very receptive anyway, and will learn 'hup' very quickly if you just raise your hand up. You can also teach them by association. Every time they happen to sit down, say 'hup' and praise them. You should rarely find it necessary physically to put a dog in the sitting position, but if you do, remember to achieve it by raising the dog's head up rather than ineffectively struggling to push his bum down.

Learning these two fundamental commands: 'come' and 'hup', as well as the very important body language that accompanies them, can be worked on naturally while the pup is still very young, before he is out of the house very much. At this stage you and the puppy are forming a close bond, and these two lessons are your way of discovering how to communicate with each other. It is like learning a language, and most pups do it as easily as a child learning to talk. Your pup is beginning to understand you – but it is a two-way process. Take time to understand your pup. What are his needs and how does he communicate them to you? What does his body language mean?

We all discover the hard way that a sudden bark for no apparent reason means: 'I need the loo, now!' But what about putting the head on one side? This is a sign that the pup is submissive and engaged with you, but also uncertain what you want. Squirming with shoulder down on the ground is also submissive – but less engaged. Squirmers often have their own agenda! Dogs use a lot of body language when communicating with each other, and you should incorporate physical signals into your training right from the start. Getting down low (as you did to teach 'come') is a welcoming sign. Raising your hand up high, almost in a Nazi-style salute, is an assertive signal, meaning 'sit up and take notice'. Later in training you will be adding lots of signals. Not only are they vital for successful handling of the dog in the field, but in years to come when your dog is a shooting-deafened old timer, you will be glad you have more than one way of communicating. Trainers can also tell a lot about novice handlers by how they are physically with their dogs. A handler who isn't very physically demonstrative is often reluctant to get stuck in when situations require, and they sometimes have a weaker bond with the dog.

By the time your pup has finished his jabs and is allowed fully out and about, the very early learning should be well enough established to carry through to the great outdoors. Don't expect too much of your pup to begin with, but you may be surprised how eager he is to do your bidding. All pups should come when you call no matter where you are. Common sense will warn you not to have the pup roaming around where there is lots of game or other wildlife. But out in the garden or in an empty field, the pup will be coming when you call every time. You can try some 'hup' exercises as well while you are playing around. Most pups get the message immediately and 'hup' just like you showed them at feed time. Don't make a big deal of either of these commands. Just insert them into your normal play and cuddles so that they become part of the game. Always praise the pup when he obeys.

Other play-learning games include playing with objects like rag-toys, rolled-up socks and tennis balls. Roll these for the pup, or give them to him, or hide them, or toss them gently. Your good pups will be obsessed with them and make strenuous efforts to get them and give them to you, no matter what. Vary this play, with throwing as the least frequent thing you do. Your aim is to get your pup to form the opinion that finding something and bringing it back to boss is the best thing ever. Most spaniel pups take very little persuading about this. If yours is slightly reluctant, you can jazz things up a bit by throwing things in the air for you to catch, and by running away from the pup to encourage him to follow you and come to you. But don't push things or make it formal.

Keep an eye on your family at this stage. Don't let them sour the pup by endlessly giving him commands or retrieves. If they have a habit of giving the pup a command and then repeating that command without the pup obeying, you will have to step in and do some family training. The golden rule that no trainer breaks is: 'Thou shalt not repeat a command'. If you get into the habit of repeating commands you are on a slippery slope that ends up with you out on the shooting field pleading with your dog: 'Come Bertie, come, there's a good boy, come back, come on, Bertie come here,' while Bertie makes his way into the next drive and everybody on the shoot winces. Even though your pup only knows two little commands, and doesn't really even think of them as commands yet, they are actually the most important commands of all. If the pup gets the message that he can ignore them, to put it bluntly, you are stuffed and that's that.

Now that he's getting out in the world, the pup will need to be on a collar and lead. Save your slip-lead for now – it's too vigorous for a little pup. Instead get a collar with a tag and a clip-on lead. Legally you are required to have a tagged collar on your dog in public. Young pups are usually quite content to toddle around alongside you on the lead. The later you leave it, the more hassle you will have. Never let even quite a young pup get into the habit of tugging you along on the lead. Just one sharp little tug and a quick 'ach, ach' is all it takes to stop it – unlike the job you would have pulling-up a fully grown Springer who has decided to drag you along. It is a similar story with heeling off the lead. Taught early on, puppies don't resent it because they naturally want to follow you around for security. This is where you can introduce the word 'heel' and then kid the pup along with you, walking him beside you. Talk to him and use your hand to keep his attention focused on you, usually by patting your thigh. Some spaniel trainers don't like to teach heeling at this early stage. Spaniels are primarily hunting dogs and many feel that heel-work learnt too early can make a spaniel sticky and reluctant to hunt in front. Use your own judgement, and in any case, don't overdo the heeling beyond what it takes to make sure the pup knows the meaning of the word.

You can definitely start introducing the whistle now. There is no mystique to whistle training, though many novices get quite hung up about it. Get yourself a load of 210 ½ whistles on cords. You will lose them and forget them, and dog-training mates will 'borrow' them, throughout your time as a dog handler – it happens to all of us. So have lots, and especially keep at least one in the

Using the 'hup' hand signal while blowing the 'stop' whistle (CHARLES SAINSBURY-PLAICE)

shooting vehicle permanently. But you don't need to be worrying about different types of whistle. 'Thunderer' whistles with a pea in them are best left for football refs and those who work pointers. As with everything in dog training, your aim is to keep it simple. Things can get quite stressful enough out there without having to worry about whistle selection. The same applies when choosing what whistle commands you will use. Most of the professionals I work with use the following:

'Peeeeep' – a long single blast to mean now stop, 'hup' and look at me. The same blast is used whether the dog is near or out working, either hunting or being directed on a blind retrieve.

'Pip, pip, pip, pip, pip' – repeated, short pipping on the whistle (usually around five pips) to mean 'come' to me.

Later in training a third whistle command will be introduced when the young dog is hunting. This whistle command is:

'Pip, pip' – just two quite little pips to tell the dog to finish his cast out and turn back towards you. This is quite a logical command, because what you are asking the dog to do is effectively 'come' part way towards you but not all the way to you.

You will meet dog handlers who use all sorts of trills and tantaras with their assortment of whistles, but we are training a dog not a concert orchestra, and you can achieve all you want – even quite complex handling on retrieves – with a combination of 'hup', 'come', and 'turn' whistles. More than this can be confusing to the dog, and to you too when things have become a little fraught. The other benefit of these very simple obvious whistle commands is that pups find them very easy and obvious to learn.

To teach the 'come' whistle (also known as the 'return'), just give your normal come command, immediately followed by 'pip, pip, pip, pip, pip' and put yourself in an inviting body position ready to welcome the incoming pup. From now on as you play, keep using all the forms of command in combination – but vary the combinations. Use the whistle then the voice, or combine a welcome position with the whistle but no verbal command. Soon you will find the pup comes quickly, whatever combination of commands you use. At this stage you can use the whistle alone and the pup will come as normal. Occasionally you may find that the pup is busy with some other activity when you call and you don't get such a good response. At this very early stage, don't think about punishing; instead think of ways to make it easier for the pup to be consistently obedient. Choose a moment when the pup happens to be looking in your direction, or is on his way towards you anyhow. When training an animal (or let's face it, managing another human!), confrontation is rarely the most effective way. So with all this 'early learning' do as much as you can to work with the pup's natural behaviours, rather than trying to force matters.

You will find that most pups instinctively stop what they are doing and look at you the first time you blow the stop whistle. Team that with the upraised hand that the puppy already knows, spit the whistle out and say 'hup'. Teaching the stop whistle is often as simple as that. Keep on training with all the three different versions of the 'hup' command at the same time i.e. verbal, hand signal and whistle. Then cease the verbal command and just use the whistle and upraised hand. Most of the time the pup will respond to this like an old pro. This is a huge step forward in your training, because even at the very top level of working your mature dog in the field, this one command 'Peeeep' and

upraised hand is how you will communicate with the dog in nearly every situation. If the dog has flushed a bird, this is how you will stop him from chasing. If a shot bird has fallen, this is how you will stop the dog from running-in. If the dog is out on a retrieve and needs directions from you, it is how you will tell him to sit up and look at you for instructions. And even more important, but much overlooked, it is how you can stop the dog from getting run over, or into all the other forms of trouble that await when out on day-to-day exercise.

When you are happy that the pup has cottoned on to this while he is close to you, try the stop whistle when he is at a distance from you, playing around the garden. Be sure not to attempt this if there are any potential distractions around. A basic patch of lawn is the easiest place. Most pups will obey naturally. But good keen hunters (our old friend 'bad pup') will be so nose down they may not notice what you have done. In this case you must choose your moment carefully. Just as he is running back within easy reach of you, blow your whistle. If he doesn't stop, reach out and grab him. Physically sit him, at the same time as blowing the stop whistle and then spitting the whistle out and saying a sharp, firm 'hup'. Repeat this a few times. When he is getting engaged with it, let him run away a bit further. Pick a moment when he is briefly looking at you, or nose up, or perhaps slightly bored. Then blow the whistle and you should get a pretty good response. If you don't, go a step back in your lessons with the original 'hupping' at feed times when he is close to you.

This is not the time for punishing a pup – particularly not a fantastic hunter that could eventually become your dog-of-a-lifetime. Later in training, if the pup is clearly giving you the 'two paws', you can think about more determined (even forceful!) ways of getting the pup's attention. For now you will get best results simply by praising and rewarding good behaviour – what psychologists call 'positive reinforcement'. Don't be tempted to give a lot of food treats. For a spaniel the best reward is your full attention and demonstrative praise. Constant food treats mean the pup gets fixated on the food, not on you. You can end up with a disastrous situation where the pup will get into the habit of spitting out retrieves because he is in so much of a hurry to get the food treat in his mouth. Remember, we want your pup bonded to you, not to a Bonio.

Throughout his life, it is better for your gundog never to have a chance to get into trouble or disobey, rather than be punished. Some top spaniels have so much drive that they regard punishment as an occupational hazard. Field

OPPOSITE: *When the dog is sat up and looking at you he is ready for a command* (CHARLES SAINSBURY-PLAICE)

43

trialling Cockers believe: 'If you can't do the time, don't do the crime'. Unfortunately they are easily hard enough to handle doing a bit of time! So you must stay one step ahead. Instead of challenging the young pup, create a situation where it is much easier for him to do the right thing than the wrong thing. So ask him to come when he is already thinking about coming back to the boss anyway. Don't tell him 'hup' just as a blackbird has flown past his nose. Stand yourself in places where you can reach the pup easily if he is going off the rails. Don't let him roam around the place unsupervised picking up bad habits. Never, ever, give a command when you are not in a position to enforce it if necessary. For example, if your pup is already in hot pursuit of a rabbit two fields away, don't blow your whistle. If the pup doesn't respond to the whistle (which he won't), there is no way even Ussein Bolt can sprint two hundred yards over rough ground to stop the dog disobeying the whistle. So now you have created a situation where the dog is not only chasing, but also disobeying the whistle. Instead don't blow the whistle, but just go and get the pup. Put him on the lead and ignore what he did. That way hopefully the penny won't drop with the pup that he has got away with something. Later in training, when steadiness is the lesson, will be the time to think of ways of dealing with chasing.

In his early puppyhood the youngster just needs to know very firmly the difference between 'happy boss' and 'cross boss'. Right from the beginning, if the puppy does something genuinely naughty, like biting or being bossy or possessive, a sharply growled 'ach, ach' is quite enough to give him the message. All pups prefer happy boss to cross boss. As long as you make it absolutely crystal clear which you are, and why, then you will get the right response. But have enough respect for your young dog to make it about him, not about you. If you are happy because you got a job promotion this week, you must still manage to be 'cross boss' when the pup does something naughty. Likewise, if you are in a bad mood because the car got clamped, and your pup is behaving beautifully, then you must be 'happy boss' with him. And no matter what disasters are happening elsewhere in life, it is surprising how quickly you will actually become a much happier boss when the pup is doing great!

TROUBLE SHOOTING

Puppy is reluctant to come
This is a real danger signal for your future relationship with the pup and the training success that depends on that relationship. The main reasons for reluctance to come are that the handler is being over-dominant, perhaps even

aggressive, or has punished a pup after he has returned to the handler, rather than on the site of the misdeed. You shouldn't be punishing at this stage anyway, and certainly never when the dog has come back to your feet. Check out your body language and tone of voice. Soften both of these. Get down on your stomach or lie on your back while happily calling the pup's name. These are very submissive postures and you will soon have pup all over you. Do something nutty to get him to come out of curiosity – run away or skip or make peculiar (but gentle) noises. But most of all, think about your own personality and your bond with the dog.

I don't seem to have a bond with the pup

Surprisingly this isn't the deal-breaker you might think. Professional gundog trainers are usually training, working and competing with other people's dogs, and it doesn't stop them building a great working relationship with a young dog they might have in the kennels for a relatively short time. I don't have a fantastic bond with all my dogs, but they all very much enjoy being part of the Gournay Court team. To form a strong bond with a dog, you must be the most important thing in his life. Dogs living in the home, rather than out in a kennel, have any number of stimulations competing to be important. They may love your kids more than they do you, or even obsessing on the tumble drier may be more fascinating than you! Be the only one to train and work your pup, and most importantly, be as interested in him as you would like him to be in you.

My pup seems quite bad tempered

Much more likely to be the case with pups living in the house, especially in large and busy families. Just as with young children, firm boundaries and a regular routine will help the pup to feel secure. Make sure the pup has his own space (kennel or indoor pen) where he can relax. Supervise family interactions with the pup for as long as necessary, and never allow children to tease the puppy. Remember to check there is no physical cause for his reactions e.g. pain from teething, umbilical hernia, worm infestation, ear mites etc.

3.
PUPPY ASSESSMENT

They may not talk about it much, but one thing the very best gundog trainers have in common is that they all think a great deal about their dogs and training plans. Competing in a field trial alongside the top handlers (whether professional or amateur) is always great fun – win or lose – because you get to spend the day chatting while you clamber about among the brambles. After an initial exchange of views on whether Man Utd or Liverpool is more likely/deserving of winning the Premiership, the talk inevitably turns to dogs. Gundog trainers are great problem solvers. If something goes wrong in a trial, they always admit it – at least to themselves, if not to their fellow competitors! Then the post mortem begins as to why things went wrong, and how the problem can be solved or avoided in future. But long before the dog has gone anywhere near a field trial, the trainer will have put in a huge amount of thinking about how he is going to get the best out of the youngster. The formal training of your pup really begins when you put the kettle on and have a bit of a think.

First assess your puppy. Ask yourself about the pup's personality and also consider what are his natural skills. In deciding when to begin the more formal training, your puppy's personality is your biggest guide, rather than any hard and fast rule about what he should be learning at six or at eight months old. Is he a bold, confident pup already getting a bit of an attitude? Is he timid and clingy, very unlikely to push the boundaries? Is he sharp, intelligent and inquisitive? Or perhaps he's a bit of a klutz, inclined to fall over his own paws. Has he picked

OPPOSITE: *Making a good bond is the most important aspect of your pup's early socialisation* (NICK RIDLEY)

up everything so far very quickly, and have the play-lessons stuck? Does the pup lack concentration? Is he a bit slow on the uptake?

With my first trialling spaniel, dear old Nancarrow 'Mad Dog' Dutch, I hadn't realised how much sitting and thinking you have to do when it comes to dogs. I just blithely assumed that since Dutch was the apple of my eye, he must certainly have the brains (if not the paws) to be a rocket scientist. After several seasons of deteriorating performances both in trials and in the shooting field, Dutch happened to be in the kitchen one evening when the telly was testing the IQ of the nation's pets. The basic entry level test was to show your dog his favourite food treat; then, still in plain view, hide it under a cup. The more intelligent the dog, the more successful he would be in getting the treat out from under the cup. I think the TV expert mentioned in passing that a small percentage of very dim pets (goldfish, gerbils etc) would be confused by the disappearance of the treat. We thought it would be fun to see how quickly brainiac Dutch, the trained working dog, would extract the treat. So we showed him the treat, and Dutch was enthused, tail wagging, ears up, in readiness to accept the choice morsel. Then we put the treat under the cup. Dutch was instantly transformed. The word crestfallen doesn't begin to describe the woebegone state radiated by every inch of Dutch's body language. 'Aw, treat gone,' he emoted, as clearly as it is possible for a dog to say, before padding dispiritedly off to his bed without even a passing glance at the cup containing his treat.

Clearly, despite being loving, willing, handsome and well bred, Dutch was a very stupid spaniel. They do exist, and in your delight at having a spaniel pup, it is easy to overlook that some are much brighter than others – and therefore that you should adjust the training accordingly. So I am constantly assessing my pups and young dogs. Most of the time it is pretty easy to spot the bright ones from the slightly challenged. Even as tiny pups, clever spaniels are the ones who are easy to wean, learning to eat from a bowl quickly. They are the first to understand what a door is, and by far the most difficult to confine when necessary. Then there are the pups who are easily confused. You come in to find them curled up fast asleep in their feed bowl – utterly charming but clearly on the wrong track! Pups change as they mature, so don't assume that one that was a little backward won't suddenly make a great leap forward. Equally, other factors may come in to mean the bright ones don't progress on an even curve. So throughout the pup's development, you must always have a thorough understanding of where he is at.

OPPOSITE: *Cockers don't always behave well on the lead!* (CHARLES SAINSBURY-PLAICE)

49

Ricky is a good example of this. When he was a very young pup I was thrilled by how quickly he was learning. But now that he is getting into the demands of formal training he is beginning to find things a bit more difficult. I think I probably rushed him a bit too much. Now that he needs to concentrate more, it is clear that his focus and attention span are still quite immature. This means I must be very thorough in how I train. I won't necessarily be asking less of him, but my approach will be very simple and steady. His lessons will be short and will concentrate on one thing at a time. I certainly won't attempt to combine the aspects of hunting, retrieving and steadiness all in one exercise until I am absolutely sure that he has really learnt each individual aspect separately. I can always tell when he is getting a bit over faced because I lose his attention and it becomes more difficult to get his eye contact.

Assessing your dog's basic intelligence and ability to learn isn't always straightforward, as the dog's inherent personality sometimes intervenes. You can have a dim dog who is so keen to please that you assume he is brighter than he is (like Dutch). Or some very bright dogs are not necessarily that committed to anything but their own agenda. One personality type that I have come across quite frequently among top trials-bred Cocker bitches is what I call the 'Uriah Heap' and which psychologists describe as passive-aggressive. My foundation bitch FTCh Abbeygale May (Tippy) is the prime example (and quite possibly to blame for many of the young versions running around today!). If you ask her to do something she doesn't want to do, like go into her kennel, she will squirm on the floor in a very submissive position, even trembling slightly. No one has ever laid a hand on her in her entire life, yet she looks for all the world like a case in urgent need of RSPCA rescue. But as soon as you click your fingers to set her off hunting, she flies off and crashes into the cover without a care.

Tippy is so bright that she has worked out she can get her own way by playing the sympathy vote. But I am wise to her now – and to her offspring! Her granddaughter, Pepper, has similar little ways. If she doesn't want to part with a retrieve, she will drop down in a cute little play bow and give me the chocolate-box look. The impulse to give in and just play with her, especially while she is still quite a little pup, is hard to overcome. But I keep an iron will. I just turn my back and refuse to give her eye contact. As soon as she realises she can't con me into playing with her, it's amazing how quickly and efficiently she brings the retrieve to hand. Understanding your own pup in this way gives you a great

OPPOSITE: *The author with eleven-year-old retired champion 'Tippy', FTCh Abbeygale May (front), and the next generation*

head start in planning your training approach and dealing with problems as they arise.

There are about four main types of spaniel you are likely to come across. Intelligent and willing is of course the best, and these days it is also the most prevalent, thanks to enlightened breeding and training over the last few decades. If you have one of these, training should be straightforward. Don't be tempted to rush the lessons though, and remember that this easy dog needs a stable environment and secure framework of rules just like any other. Another type is the equally intelligent, but rather naughty spaniel – although sometimes, perceived naughtiness is connected with inexperienced handling. These dogs often make up into the ones who will really take you to the heights in your gundog work. Be firm and fair. Consistency is an absolute must in training this kind of dog. Where a bright dog who is basically on your side will give you the benefit of the doubt, the clever but self-motivated dog will try to exploit your weaknesses. Don't have any! Never let him get away with a thing – but praise him loads when he does well, especially if he has had to do something against the grain. Eventually you will gain his respect and have fantastic years ahead of working together.

Another type of spaniel is every bit as willing as our 'perfect pup', but unfortunately lacking in grey matter. Your 'nice-but-dim' pup is sadly never going to be a field trial champion, but still has a great future as a wonderful dog to shoot over – if you get the training right. Take it slowly, be patient, and always make every lesson easy for the dog to achieve. Never let 'nice-but-dim' get into high stress situations where he can go wrong. The most unfortunate spaniel type, which you very occasionally come across, is the one that is all-round ignorant – both thick and with a bad attitude, known in the old days as a 'hard' dog. Toffee was dim as brick and not especially willing to make an effort. I suspected trouble because he never gave me eye contact. Normally there is little a spaniel likes doing better than gazing lovingly into the eyes of his boss (in a way no spouse ever does, from the engagement onwards). A succession of gundog friends, both amateur and professional, tried to get on terms with Toffee. The results were discouraging until we found a Scottish grouse keeper who wanted a wild spaniel with a lot of stamina to run round madly putting up grouse coveys for him to count. This rather specialist occupation has proved the ideal billet for Toffee to show his fortunately rare aptitude!

The fifth type of spaniel is one that seems to crop up fairly frequently with Cockers, and can best be described as 'the clown'. This dog is somewhere between 'perfect pup' and 'bright but naughty'. The squirming 'Uriah Heap' is definitely in the clown category, and a lot of top field trial Cockers do seem

Seize the moment when the pup happens to sit and set up an association by giving the command 'hup' and hand signal (NICK RIDLEY)

to have a very active sense of humour. Wendy Openshaw ran FTCh Mallowdale Rackateer for several seasons with great success and he was a brilliant dog. But whenever she sat him down at her feet, perhaps waiting to be sent on a retrieve, he had a way of craning his head and neck round to look up at her without moving his body. The effect was so comically exaggerated it just had to be a mickey-take – and he never let his little joke affect the quality of his work. Jon Bailey was close to winning a rabbit trial one very hot day up in the Highlands of Scotland. The dog was on its way back with a retrieve when he came across a cool, clear little burn flowing across his path. He carefully put the rabbit down on a nearby flat stone, and then went for a refreshing swim, before picking up the rabbit again and resuming his journey back to Jon – who was by now waiting to put his lead on while the rest of us collapsed laughing. My own Cockers seem to be able to keep everyone amused – though not necessarily me . . . . It is a character trait which you just have to put up with while remaining as consistent and firm in your training as you are with 'bright but naughty' pup. One excellent technique for getting the better of a clown is for him not to get a laugh. If he realises his joke has fallen flat he doesn't often repeat it. The only trouble is trying to keep a straight face, because Cockers can be pretty good comedians!

When assessing your spaniel and planning his formal training, the other major factor to take into account is what job you want him to do when he graduates. Few novice handlers give enough thought to this. The trend among shooting folk is to assume that any trained gundog can do anything on the shooting field. The Edwardians would have been horrified at this, and even until comparatively recently it was understood that a dog cannot be expected to be perfect at all the many and varied aspects of gundog work. A hundred years ago every breed had its specific function. Labrador retrievers were used for picking up game behind the line. Original Labrador bloodlines (like the famous and most ancient, the Buccleuch) were favoured by gentlemen Guns to sit on the peg. Flat-coat retrievers were also fashionable as peg dogs, largely because of their impressive looks. Rabbits were shot over Cocker Spaniels, and Cockers were also popular on grouse moors because of their stamina and ability to cope with heat. Springer Spaniels were used mainly by keepers and beaters to hunt and flush game. Rough shooters began to work them as 'all-rounders' but until comparatively recently no serious Gun shooting driven game would even consider having a Springer sitting on his peg.

So every dog had his day and wasn't expected to do one thing one day and something completely different the next day – or the next drive. It is a bitter pill to swallow, but the Edwardians were essentially right! No dog which is used in the beating line in the first drive, then picking up behind the line on the second drive, can be expected to remain rock steady on the peg throughout the third drive. I'm sorry, but there it is. The worst gundog work I ever see in the field is on stand-and-walk shoots. Dogs dash around wildly in the beating line, often chasing a bird right through the cover and on beyond the flushing point – pausing only in their mad career to pick up the shot bird and then run off with it. Dogs are sat on pegs after they have been allowed – even encouraged – to commit all manner of sins on the previous drive, and naturally they run in like Wayne Rooney celebrating a goal.

As a guest on one of these wild dog shoots, I stupidly brought a champion trials dog with me. After she'd had a retrieve actually ripped out of her mouth by a German Short-Haired Pointer who appeared at speed from who knows where, I quietly retired her to the back of the vehicle. If only I could have retreated into the Landcruiser with her! So, if you enjoy this book and find it helpful, promise me one thing: please, don't let your young spaniel become an all-round hooligan.

The first step in avoiding this dreadful outcome is to analyse your own shooting habits. What kind of shooting do you do most? Are you an 'urban Gun' who does most of his shooting from the peg on large, commercial driven shoots? If so, you must understand that you are going against the grain of what a spaniel is historically intended to do. Spaniels are naturally hunters, rather than peg dogs. You can have success, but your training must be adjusted accordingly – right from this moment onwards. At the time of writing we are in the middle of a perverse fashion for having Cockers as peg dogs. My own Cockers do come and sit on the peg with me – but only once they are thoroughly retired from their trialling days (the older the better!). Trying to have a fit, young, hard-hunting Cocker with bags of drive sitting on your peg is slightly more exasperating than taking your three-year-old son with you round the January sales. If this is what your heart is set on, put this book aside, go on the internet and buy a retired Cocker from one of the top field triallers, then relax.

The good news though, is that it is only in this one area of the peg dog on the four hundred-bird driven shoot, that using a spaniel isn't really advisable. In every other aspect of work in the field – rough shooting, picking-up, beating, occasional peg-sitting – I would opt for a spaniel every time. Recognise your main sphere, and adjust the training accordingly. If you mainly pick up, then concentrate on retrieving and steadiness rather than worrying too much about getting a lot of drive and style into the dog's hunting work. A keen rough shooter, on the other hand, will want his dog to hunt with accuracy and flair;

so getting that right will take priority over the retrieving. Those who like to go beating will need a hard-hunting, fit dog, but he won't be called on to do much retrieving. Beaters should also remember that maintaining steadiness is going to be a huge issue. Working in the beating line is, of all activities, the most likely to unsteady your dog. And if you really are determined that your spaniel is going to be purely a peg dog, then you don't have to worry about teaching hunting or retrieving. But this book will still come in useful. You can close it, put it down on the floor, and spend the next two years getting your spaniel to sit motionless beside it.

All my spaniels are initially trained with field trialling in mind. A field trial is really just an organised version of rough shooting. The spaniel is required to hunt a specific area (the beat), entering cover readily and missing no ground. When he finds game, he must flush or bolt the game, and sit steadily (drop to flush) while the game is shot. On a command from his handler he must then retrieve the fallen game to hand. It is all very straightforward – hunt, flush, be steady, retrieve – except that no little hiccups are allowed! A little dash forward after the flush or the shot, and you're out of the trial. Mess around and fail to retrieve the game, and you're out. Pull on ahead out of easy range for the Guns, and you're out. This is exactly what a spaniel is born and bred to do. It is rough shooting – but as it would be on a perfect day!

For this rough shooting-plus-a-bit career, excellent hunting is a priority, so this is what I will be encouraging the pup to enjoy. Retrieving can take a little bit of a back seat, and absolute steadiness will come later in the programme when I am convinced about the youngster's hunting drive and confidence. Once you have decided which is going to be your pup's major aim, read the next three chapters in the appropriate order. I have laid them out for rough shooting/ trialling dogs as follows: hunting, retrieving, steadiness. But for mainly pickers-up read them: retrieving, hunting, steadiness. For peg dogs read steadiness first. Beaters can look at hunting, then steadiness, then retrieving.

Your dog's temperament will eventually influence which aspect you spend most time on. An excellent natural hunter with a lot of drive will need to do quite a bit of work on steadiness to learn to curb his enthusiasm. A sticky, timid hunter will learn steadiness almost too quickly, so be careful not to overdo those lessons. Keep adjusting as you go along. Teach the exercises separately – putting it all together comes later on.

OPPOSITE: *The author shooting over Ricky, whose peg dog training is now complete*

Your puppy's training begins now, but he shouldn't be aware of it! (NICK RIDLEY)

Now you can give your pup a little assessment test to see if he's ready to begin structured training. This will offer a more accurate insight than just sticking to the 'around six months old' formula. Go out into the garden, or field. Choose somewhere with no game and few distractions. If it also has a bit of rough grass – or even a flower bed – so much the better. Take the puppy off the lead and let him run round and let off a bit of steam. Is he straight into the flower bed nose down? Excellent. That means he is a natural hunter. He has passed the first question with flying colours. Does he linger round you and just potter about a bit? This isn't exactly a fail, but tells you he's a softer dog and you will need to work on getting him going in his hunting.

Next use your whistle to call the dog to you. If he comes immediately, straight to your feet with no hesitation, that's a pass – and if he did it from nose down in the bushes that's an A*. If he doesn't come, go up to him and pull him towards you while pipping the whistle. Then choose a moment when he's not doing much, is near you, or has half his attention on you. He should come easily this time. If he doesn't, that's a fail, and he's not ready to go to the next stage of training.

If he's passed everything so far, pop him on the lead and let him see you throw his toy, tennis ball, whatever. Don't give him a command but just take him off the lead and see what happens. A dash out and return to your feet with the retrieve is another A*. If he goes out, picks up the retrieve, but needs return pipping before he comes back to you, that's a pass. If he runs away quite determinedly with the retrieve, don't worry too much. Just run off in the opposite direction and he'll soon bring it back. Things to worry about are not showing an interest in the object, despite having seen it clearly, or trying to eat it, or not chasing you to give it back. This is a clear sign not to proceed with retrieving training. You should also suspect that either you or other family members have been throwing the pup too many retrieves and you have soured it. You can still go ahead with hunting work, and that will often work wonders when you next try the retrieve test.

The final test is to check your pup's aptitude for the third of its future trio of skills – steadiness. Remember you are not looking for the pup actually to be steady at this early stage, but it can show you how ready he is to accept steadiness. First of all hup your pup. With hand raised in the hup command position, gradually back away from him. I find that backing off in a spiralling path works well. If he continues to sit and watches you, that's wonderful – especially if he was previously hunting the flower bed – again another A* performance, and one that says you have created an excellent bond of mutual trust between you and your pup already. If he gets up and follows you, that's fine. At least 80 per cent of pups will do this initially and it isn't a failure. What is a fail though, is if he gets up and wanders off elsewhere without giving you a passing glance. You haven't yet established a strong enough bond with your pup to be able to take on more complex training.

For a pup that has scored straight As so far, there is a final test. Let him set off and get his nose down. Then blow your stop whistle and hold up your hand in the hup position. If he stops immediately and sits up to look at you, then rejoice. You have an A* trainable pup with every chance of maturing into a really good dog. You and the pup should award each other a huge cuddle, tomorrow you start training proper! But definitely don't write off the moderate pup at this stage. The average pass is by far the most likely, and this pup too can go on to structured training. With the pup that hasn't quite managed to achieve these early goals yet, don't be worried. Just slow down a bit. Keep on with the play-training; address any specific issues you have discovered; then try the test again in a week or so. Don't ever repeat the test on the day. It is not a training exercise, merely a way of assessing your dog's development.

TROUBLE SHOOTING

My pup doesn't seem to be catching on very quickly
Most of the time poor learning is due to some external factor. Is there too much going on around the pup? Too many people playing with him? Are you spending enough one-on-one time with him? Are you rushing him? Above all you must remember to be very clear, simple and consistent in everything you do with the pup.

The puppy is getting very boisterous and jumping up a lot
Good for him! This generally means he's ready to get more serious about training. Be firm, don't punish, but do praise good behaviour. With an excitable dog praise him gently and calmly, using voice more than physical touch. Jumping up is endemic to Cockers – all professional trainers can be spotted by their muddy thighs! But try to avoid a Springer getting this habit. Turn your back on him, then hup him and make him sit calm for a moment. Don't be tempted to whack down a jump-up pup as it can make them a bit hand-shy.

My puppy is getting a bit snappy
Make sure no one is giving him food treats or playing tug-of-war with him, or teasing him in any way. If he snaps tick him off firmly with a harsh, gruff voice and turn your back on him. Most pups grow out of this fairly quickly.

His concentration seems quite poor
Use lots of ten-minute play-lessons rather than one long one. Gently but firmly insist he listens to you. Have his favourite toy in your pocket and be the person to control whether he gets it or not, this way you will become the centre of what little attention he has! Get him out and about so that he gets used to new things and isn't so distracted by them. Don't rush from one lesson to another. Really insist on the feed bowl lesson so that he gets into the habit of sitting and thinking about one thing.

4.
HOW TO HUNT

Before you start training your young spaniel to hunt, bear in mind that there is very little of it about these days. With the marked dominance of driven or semi-driven shooting, rather than genuine rough shooting, it is quite rare to see spaniels hunting correctly in the shooting field. So rare, in fact, that if you are a first-time spaniel handler, I'm willing to bet you haven't actually watched the real thing. You may think you have, but in all likelihood what you have seen is just wild spaniels rushing round madly with the beaters, or zooming about equally chaotically after runners with the pickers-up. You may even have been 'rough shooting' with a spaniel-owning friend – the pair of you walking faster and faster trying to keep within range of birds being flushed ever further away, by a spaniel that simply runs on in front. Take it from me, there is an awful lot more to it than that. No matter what your opinion of field trialling, I recommend strongly that you get yourself to a spaniel field trial in order to see how hunting should be done. Whether or not you ever compete with your dog, or even let anyone other than yourself shoot over it, you still need to know the kind of thing you are aiming at. If you don't understand just how close to the Gun a spaniel should hunt in order for that Gun to get an easy shot, you will be forever wondering why shooting over your dog is such an unrewarding sport.

Many of my non-trialling shooting friends have been co-opted into coming out and shooting over my spaniels, and they have all found it to be a revelation. 'It's amazing the way the dog just stops dead like that so you can get a clear shot at the rabbit,' said one friend, who'd been rough shooting for years. Duh! The whole point of training your spaniel to be shot over is to make the shooting as easy and efficient as possible. Another friend conceded: 'I always thought you had to be fit to go rough shooting – you know, all that running to keep up with the dog – but your dogs seem to go at the same pace I do.' Again, duh! So go to a spaniel field trial. You will also meet lots of really helpful and well-informed spaniel trainers who may become life-long friends. I competed in my first novice trial, basically to provide the comic relief, knowing absolutely nothing. I finished the day knowing a lot of wonderful people and a little bit more about dog training. Spaniel people are great, so if you don't already, get to know some. Ask your shoot, the local gamekeeper, and go online. The Kennel Club has a list of all the different field trialling clubs with contact details, so you can easily find one near you (See Appendix III).

There is a lot more to a field trial than just hunting, but for a spaniel, good hunting is really important. What you will see is the dog quartering (zig-zag-ging) in front of its handler, and a Gun walking on either side of the handler, about ten metres away on either side. When you are training, there won't be Guns beside you (until the very last lessons). The dog should go approximately fifteen metres to one side of the handler before turning back towards the handler, passing in front of him, and going fifteen metres out to the other side. The avenue thus created is about thirty metres wide, and is known as the 'beat'. The imaginary track a dog makes as he is quartering is called the 'pattern'. Pattern is all-important for good hunting. Many gundog training manuals go into elaborate detail about pattern when quartering, with complicated geometric diagrams. I read these books before I went trialling, but although I am academic and bookish, I am afraid all the squiggly diagrams weren't a patch on looking at the real thing. If you can't get to a trial, buy a DVD or video. Paul French films the Springer and Cocker championships every year and you can get a DVD or video by ordering online (See Appendix III).

The reason for pattern in quartering is not just to perform clever zig-zags or even complicated figures-of-eight. The primary function of the pattern is to hunt thoroughly and efficiently all the cover in front of the Guns without miss-ing any ground or any of the game which may be hiding there. Once found, the game needs to be flushed close to the Guns, so that they have plenty of time to shoot it before it gets out of range. When you think of it this way, working out the correct pattern is just a matter of common sense.

It is important to have a thorough understanding of how hunting works for a spaniel. Good spaniels rely pretty much exclusively on their scenting ability in order to find game, whether living, wounded or dead. Since this is the one sense that humans very rarely use, it can be hard to 'think dog'. Watch your pup closely as he bombs about the place. You may see his head turn suddenly, as if

Don't slow down a stylish hunter, but make sure he stays on the whistle (NICK RIDLEY)

he has seen something out of the corner of his eye. In fact he has scented something out of the corner of his nose, and he is turning his nose into the wind in order to smell it better. For a dog, nose comes first among the sensory input, and it is always the one he will trust first. Where humans say they 'couldn't believe their eyes' about something surprising, dogs would say 'they couldn't believe their nose'.

Scent is mainly carried in moisture molecules in the air, or on the ground. Air-borne scent is carried by the wind towards or away from the dog's nose, depending which way the wind is blowing. So when thinking about pattern, the common sense is that we want the dog to be hunting in such a way that he gets as much of the air-carried scent into his nose as possible. Therefore the dog should be quartering into the wind which is carrying that scent. You will see when good spaniels are hunting that they always make their turns into the wind.

63

Sometimes the wind may be blowing in a different direction from the one we want to hunt, and again common sense dictates that we have to adjust the pattern to take this into account, so that we still get as much wind as possible into the dog's nostrils. It isn't about making fancy patterns on the ground (or even diagrams in a book); it's about the dog's nose being exposed to the maximum amount of scent. If the wind is coming from behind him and he is working away from that direction, he won't get as much scent as if he were working back into the wind.

Wind and scent can be confusing though, particularly since it's not instinctive to humans. I like to think of the wind as a river flowing along, with the scent being a leaf carried by the current. If the river/wind is flowing towards you, it's easy, the leaf/scent will come to you. But if the river current is flowing away from you, then the leaf/scent is getting further from you, which means you (that is, the dog) must go and get it. Air currents can flow across you from one side or the other as well, so this too needs to be taken into account. When the air is flowing towards you, we call it working into the wind, and this is the easiest way to hunt your dog. If the air is blowing away from you, that's a back wind, and much tougher to hunt. If the air is being blown from one side or the other, it's known as a 'cheek wind' for the obvious reason that you can feel it against one cheek or the other.

From now onwards you are going to need to be very aware of scenting conditions and where the wind is coming from whenever you work your dog. It is of the utmost importance for him, and so you have to get expert in it as well. What makes life harder for humans is that it's not always easy for us to tell where the wind is coming from, although to dogs it's obvious (because that's where all the juicy smells are coming from!). My first champion, FTCh Kelm-scott Whizz (Lynn), who was originally trained by top trials judge and championship winner Steve Wanstall, had an absolute mastery of the wind. A back wind especially (blowing away from us), she would hunt in a sensible, but to a novice handler, rather worrying, pattern. To begin with she would run in a straight line away in front of me for about fifteen or twenty metres. Just as I was panicking, thinking, 'she's pulling on too far, she's getting away from me and the Guns', she would turn round and hunt her way back towards me, quartering into the wind and getting maximum scent. This had the added bonus that the birds she flushed tended to fly towards the Guns, a much easier shot – making for lots of dead birds and nice simple retrieves. Lynn was an old pro by the time I had her, and her attitude was clearly 'birds in the game bag, job done'.

Following Lynn's logic, with a cheek wind (coming from the side), the dog should run out to the extreme edge of his beat before then turning and quartering his way into the cheek wind, moving across at right angles to the line of handler and guns, until he reaches the opposite side of the beat. Then he would run (not hunting), in a straight line back again to the original edge of the beat (now about fifteen metres further up the beat) and start the whole process once more. Few dogs and fewer handlers are capable of this sort of precision. But the general idea holds good – work the beat in such a way that you get the maximum amount of scent without missing any ground. So don't be slavish about your zigs and your zags, just make sure the dog is covering all the ground with its nose into the wind as much as possible. Watch your dog very closely. Most spaniels are instinctively good hunters, and apart from keeping them always well within shot range, you shouldn't try to interfere with their natural pattern too much.

All this does presuppose, though, that you know where the wind is coming from in the first place. You will see people tossing grass into the air knowledgeably, which is a shame, because they are often throwing it in the opposite direction from the way the wind is going! Professional big game hunters in Africa, whose lives sometimes depend on knowing which way the wind is blowing, have little squeegee bottles to puff out tiny clouds of fine ash or talcum powder into the air. On the stillest of days, the cloud hangs for a second before very gently drifting away in the direction the wind is blowing. You don't need to go to those lengths, but never assume you know the wind. Be aware of it in a number of different ways. Which way are the clouds moving? That tells you high level wind direction and wind strength. Which way are the trees blowing? If they are swirling or being blown in the opposite direction from the clouds, that means a changeable wind and difficult scenting conditions. If there is long grass, which way is it being bent? That tells you about low level wind, the most important for your dog. Feel the wind on your face and hands. Does one side of you feel warmer than the other? That side is in the lee of the wind. Turn away from your warm side, and you should feel what wind there is in your face. Some people like to hold up a licked finger, but personally all that has ever told me is that I have a wet hand.

Wind can change while you are working the dog, and it can even be different in different parts of the ground you are working. Thermal air currents funnelling upwards on the edge of a steep hill-side, which you will often find on upland ground out rabbiting or grouse shooting, can cause havoc with wind direction. A similar effect occurs on the edges of large woods – just where you are hunting for pheasants. So every time you take your lead off, be wind aware, and stay

65

wind aware throughout the time your dog is working – whether it is hunting or retrieving. And always trust your dog's nose above your own. If he is constantly wanting to work in a particular way, and he isn't just dashing around being naughty, go with his flow. Too many times I have taken a dog away from game without knowing it, just because I thought he was losing his pattern.

So now you understand the art of hunting, time to start putting it into practice with your puppy. You will already know by now if he is a keen natural hunter, in which case all you need to do is add a bit of control and discipline into his work. Choose a dampish, cool day to begin with and find some ground that has light cover (no thick brambles at this stage) where you will always be able to see the dog. If the ground has had game on it, great – but make sure there isn't any there now. It's amazing how an apparently empty piece of ground can be teeming with life! I have come across roe deer and even a sleeping racehorse while training. If you think there may be rabbits or perhaps the odd cock pheasant about, either use a trained dog to clear the ground, or walk round yourself. Be sure the pup doesn't see any of this happening.

Walk the pup on the lead to the area you have decided on as your beat. Check the wind. Make life easy by working the dog into the wind, so be sure the wind is blowing towards you and towards the area you want the dog to work. Take the pup off the lead, but don't let him dash off hunting immediately as he would in play. Let him hup for a moment. Then tell him 'get on' and bend down and gesture out to one side with your hand. Some handlers like to click their fingers. Keep your hand as low as possible. This encourages the dog to get his nose down, and tells him you are not throwing a retrieve or making direction signals. Nine times out of ten your pup will 'get on' without hesitation, rushing off in the general direction you gestured with nose down. Many youngsters need little further help after that, quartering naturally into the scent and staying fairly close to you. Cockers especially, while not so great at retrieving, seem to have an in-bred pattern, flashing around busily in front of you and weaving their way sinuously through the cover. As bigger dogs, Springers have a tendency to be bounding away with a lot of drive, but rapidly getting too far away or missing ground.

Once the pup has got going and is starting to hunt quite fluently, you will probably need to tighten up his pattern a bit. You may notice he is too far ahead of you in each sweep he makes, or he might be running out in straight lines instead of quartering in zig-zags. Another common problem is a dog that goes too far out at the sides of the beat. Now you need to teach him the turn whistle. Start by giving him the recall whistle of rapid pipping. When he comes to you, just acknowledge his return briefly, before sending him out hunting again to the other side of you. Remember to keep your hand gesture low and close to you. Do this a couple of times. Then put him on the lead and walk to heel for a breather. Next start him hunting again. As soon as he has gone just four or five metres from you, blow the turn whistle – simply a gentle 'pip, pip'. Don't blow more than two pips, and keep it as unobtrusive as possible. The idea is that the dog will eventually be turning naturally without a lot of frantic blowing from you. As soon as he hears the whistle the pup will assume he is returning and start coming towards you. Let him come in, but don't make him stop. Instead send him straight out hunting on the other side in a single, smooth movement. Pups catch onto this very quickly and soon learn to distinguish between the quiet 'pip, pip' of a turn whistle and the more insistent, rapid 'pip, pip, pip, pip, pip' of a return whistle.

Be sure that your pup gets into the habit of crossing very close to you when he goes past in front of you. A lot of top handlers like to have the dog run almost over their boots as they cross. This is really important in the case of a strong dog with a lot of hunting drive. If you let him cross a metre in front of you, he will soon be dashing past three metres ahead of you, with clouds of pheasants bursting up miles out of range. If you want to cover the ground more quickly or take in more of it, you can always move forward more. It is really important to keep spaniels close when they are quartering, and not insisting on it is a bad habit I often notice myself falling into. It's alarming just how quickly things can get out of hand with just a little slippage.

Leading trainers have lots of techniques they use to keep this nice, tight pattern. John Cook carries a small dummy in his bag. When the dog isn't looking, he slides it gently to the ground down beside his foot. Then he steps backwards away from the dummy while blowing the turn whistle. As the dog turns to come past John, he 'finds' the dummy almost at John's feet, a great reward, and this encourages the dog always to come really close past John – just in case it might find something again. This does have an excellent 'tightening' effect on a dog's pattern, as long as you can get the knack of dropping the dummy without the pup seeing, and then stepping *backwards* away from it – you don't want the dog to get in the habit of hunting behind you. Ian Flint is a great believer in using your hand. Gundogs become very hand aware and will be keen to come and put their nose where your hand is. So Ian moves his hand or clicks his fingers down low by his boots and this is very effective.

If your pup isn't getting the hang of zig-zags you can walk diagonally yourself. Even when just exercising young pups, I always tend to wander about in

Use a low hand signal when telling the dog to 'get on' and hunt
(CHARLES SAINSBURY-PLAICE)

loops and zig-zags. It encourages the pups to be stylish – as well as keeping them guessing about what I'm going to do next! Do remember to be aware of the wind though, and don't start going the wrong way. Watch your pup closely. True scenting ability is instinctive, not learnt. If your pup is constantly turning a particular way that you don't want, first check to find out whether it might be the wind and the scent causing him to behave as he is doing. In this one issue, there may actually be times where the young dog is right and you are wrong.

Some youngsters are more timid about their hunting. If they don't want to get stuck in, you must make it all more appealing and exciting. Be sure to work on a day with good scent, and try to find ground that has plenty of scent on it.

For a sticky hunter it helps if you can get into a pheasant release pen once there are no more than one or two birds left in it. With a hard-going youngster it would be a disaster to have a flush at this stage, but with a timid pup it could be just the boost it needs. One of my youngsters, who became a top champion, actually turned tail and ran the first time she flushed a cock pheasant! So a bit of uncontrolled action doesn't need to be the end of the world for a soft pup. If you have access to a rabbit pen, that's also helpful, but make sure you keep the youngster away from any chance of actually catching (pegging) a rabbit – and be wary that many rabbit pen rabbits are quite tame.

Another way of encouraging a reluctant hunter is to let him see a retrieve at the start of his hunting. While the youngster is still on the lead, gently toss a dummy a little way into the cover. Don't let the pup have the retrieve, but walk forward and pick it up yourself – making sure that you walk between the dog and the dummy, so that the dog is unsighted and doesn't realise that you have actually picked up the dummy yourself. Surreptitiously put the dummy back into your bag or pocket. Then return to the dog, let him off the lead and tell him 'get on' to start hunting. Thinking the retrieve is still there to be found, even non-hunters will be enthused and start hunting vigorously. I suspect that these kinds of tricks have been used by gundog trainers for ever – I wonder if this is where the phrase 'let the dog see the rabbit' comes from.

In general as trainers, we do need to let our young dogs 'see the rabbit' a bit. In our anxiety to bring on a steady dog, we often shelter our young pups too much, so that situations in the field can come as a bit of a shock to both dog and handler. With peg dogs of course, steadiness is at an absolute premium. But when training a rough-shooting or all-rounder spaniel, you need hunting drive and retrieving flair just as much as steadiness. Shooting over a stodgy spaniel that has had all the flair trained out of him can be very boring.

So if your young spaniel is beginning to show a bit of style in his hunting, try to go with the flow as far as possible. But you do need brakes! Once you are happy with the pup's hunting, bring in some of your early obedience exercises. Blow the stop whistle. He should drop instantly, just as he always has done. If he doesn't, jog up to him, gently drag him to where he was when you blew the whistle, sit him up and blow the whistle again. After a couple of lessons you should be able to stop him at will when he is hunting. If his obedience has gone out of the window through his excitement at hunting, you need to go back a stage and do more obedience work and less hunting. Once the dog has responded to the stop whistle, he will be hupped (usually about five to ten metres away) looking at you and wondering what to do next. You can then ask

69

Encourage him to get into all the cover (CHARLES SAINSBURY-PLAICE)

him to do one of three things: return to you; stay while you walk up to him; or carry on hunting. While training, make sure you are unpredictable in which one of these commands you give. Don't let him carry on hunting every time, or he won't bother stopping when you blow the whistle. Conversely, if you call him to you every time, he will come straight back even though you have only blown the stop whistle. And once you have tested the brakes successfully, don't be pestering the hunting dog with it all the time or he will get sticky, either through boredom or loss of confidence.

Obviously, by blowing the stop whistle you are simulating the moment in the field when the dog has flushed or bolted game and must drop to the flush instantly. The temptation for a youngster to chase at this moment is almost overwhelming, so you are going to need those brakes when the day comes that he has his first flush. That's a little way off, but remember, if he doesn't stop 100 per cent on the whistle now, when there is no live game around, he certainly isn't going to stop with a bunny's rear-end in front of his nose. Nor should you get the idea that just because he does stop on the whistle while practice hunting, that means he is 'steady'. Obeying the whistle is simply obedience. A thoroughly steady dog is one who drops at the flush, shot and fall of game without any further command from its handler. As you go on with training you will discover that 100 per cent obedience translates to as little as 10 per cent genuine steadiness in the field – and anything less than 100 per cent obedience rapidly degenerates to complete wildness when the pheasants are flying!

So, even though your youngster is hunting well and staying obedient, we still need to control the kind of temptation we let him have. Introducing retrieving into the hunting situation is the next step to bring him nearer to field conditions. It will help us to simulate many of the jobs we expect the dog to do in the field, all the way from remaining steady to a bolting rabbit (or rolled tennis ball), to remaining sat under a rain of pheasants (dummies). We can also lay our retrieves in such a way as not just to mimic real shooting life, but improve the dog's hunting performance. So now it's time to get serious with your young spaniel's retrieving exercises.

TROUBLE SHOOTING

My pup doesn't seem to have a very good sense of smell
He does, of course, it's something like 10,000 times more strongly developed than ours! Are you trying to work him somewhere that has very strong smells (diesel fumes, sheep, chemicals etc) that are spoiling his scenting? Or perhaps you are working him in very poor scenting conditions – dry, hot, no wind or simply no scent. Many very good spaniels don't bother to hunt if they know there is nothing to find. You could try planting some dummies etc in the cover in advance to give him something, or take him somewhere that has had pigeons feeding or similar.

As soon as I start my pup hunting he just dashes off
Lay off the hunting exercises a little while longer until he matures and becomes

a bit more bonded to you. Then start your hunting again, this time using the dummy as described in the chapter to keep him nearer you and more interested in you. A well-bonded pup has an invisible elastic between you and him which is stretched during hunting, but never snapped. If he isn't even obeying the whistle, then you have to go back to the early obedience lessons for a while. Try to work out where he is dashing off to – could there be a chicken shed a couple of fields away? Or is he simply running down a back wind? Be really aware of your surroundings, we can sometimes overlook quite basic answers to problems.

The pup hunts OK but doesn't seem to cover all the ground

This is the most common fault of inexperienced dogs. Don't be too anxious yourself to walk forward quickly and rush him. Let him take his time to work out the cover. Use your hand and verbal encouragement to get his nose into thicker areas. Make sure you always train in easy scenting conditions: into the wind, on a cool, damp day with a bit of wind, on ground that has a little game scent. Don't try to over-command him and force him into a pattern. Instead encourage him to work it out for himself as much as possible and he will improve with experience.

He won't get on and hunt but just hangs round me all the time

This isn't necessarily a sign of timidness, but may mean that the pup has an especially strong bond with you. If you have been, stop throwing retrieves for your pup. Instead start rolling tennis balls for him to chase. Hide stuff around the ground for him to come across, apparently unconnected with you. If you or a friend have an older, trained dog this is one occasion where you can let the youngster go off hunting with him. Eventually the pup will start finding all this more exciting than being with you, and then you can re-commence conventional training. It is often the way with problems that you have to think outside the box for a while, but once the problem is solved you should go back to tried and tested methods.

5.
THE RIGHT ROAD TO RETRIEVING

The first thing to do when you start training retrieving is: stop throwing retrieves! Standing around chucking a lot of dummies for the pup to hoover up is all very well, and I'm sure both you and he are feeling jolly pleased with yourselves – but how much have you really achieved? Indeed, it's rather missing the point to assume you have to train retrieving in the first place. Almost any dog can find and retrieve something he wants without your help – whether it be last night's take-away left-overs; a cache of illegal drugs; the contents of next door's rubbish bin; or indeed a small canvas dummy. So the objective of retrieve training isn't simply bringing stuff back. It's all about when *not* to bring stuff back; *what* to bring back; and *when* to bring it back.

The day the young dog starts dummy work (loosely called retrieving) is the first time you are asking him to do a real job for you – i.e. find and fetch the dummy. Up until now the training has been all about learning to communicate with each other (the commands and the whistle) while the dog is basically enjoying himself in a fairly unstructured way, either just playing around or out hunting. Now you are going to put your ability to communicate to the test in a more demanding situation. By using the dummies in several different ways (hiding, more than one dummy etc) you will be giving the pup new challenges. Throughout these challenges you want the pup to remain calm, sensible – and above all, responsive to you and your commands. When you think about it from this angle, it becomes obvious that the last thing you as a trainer should do is throw a dummy in the air in plain view and let the dog go and get it. This is just 'park life'. Watch people with tennis ball launchers or frisbees at your local park and you will see the dogs get more and more over-excited until their brains are in melt-down. Not what should be happening to your young, soon-to-be-perfect, gundog.

Ian Openshaw uses his whistle while handling a dog on a retrieve
(CHARLES SAINSBURY-PLAICE)

Ian Openshaw, one of the most successful of all professional spaniel trainers in the last twenty years, almost never throws a retrieve for a young dog. He explains: 'There is a lot of talk about how you must keep a dog steady by picking up nine out of ten retrieves yourself. Some gundog trainers will sit a dog up and walk in a circle throwing dummies and picking them up. It is called a marked retrieve when you sit a dog up, throw a dummy in the air, let it fall in full view, and then send the dog. A marked retrieve is the easiest possible retrieve for a young gundog, and any halfway decent youngster will find it so laughably easy you might just as well go and pick it up yourself for all the value it has as a training exercise! I very rarely actually throw a marked retrieve for a dog in the first place, which means I don't have to go round picking them up again myself! It isn't a question of steadiness either. If the dog stops on the whistle, it stops on the whistle and that's that. You don't need to go round picking up dummies to prove the point. After all, we are training the dog to work for us, not the other way round.'

I have taken Ian's words to heart and been very successful following his methods. There have been some additional benefits as well. Firstly, it is obvious to us all that throwing a lot of easy 'marked' retrieves for a dog tends to over-excite him, so you then have to work harder on the steadiness. Hence the picking-up nine out of ten dummies yourself. But with spaniels, it can also bore the young dog. Spaniels are by nature keen hunters, and may not be that bothered about retrieving – certainly not something as bland and uninteresting as a green canvas dummy (although it's a different story when it's a bunny legging it over the horizon!). This was apparent when I started training the young Springer, Ricky, on dummies. The easier the retrieve, the less enthused he was. But I wasn't alarmed by this, because I knew I wouldn't be throwing many 'marked' retrieves anyway. Since I began the challenging dummy exercises, Ricky has been transformed. I will let him see me hide a dummy in long grass beside a path, tell him 'leave it', and then we both walk away from the dummy up the path. Eventually I will stop, turn round back in the direction of the dummy, hup Ricky and then send him off for the dummy with the command: 'get out'. He never forgets where the dummy is, and is out and back with it like lightning, very full of enthusiasm for a job well done. As an experiment I have even left a dummy overnight, and Ricky has found it without difficulty.

You can start even quite a young pup with this exercise, and it can be performed either with or without the use of the lead, depending on how well your pup is heeling. Walk along with the dog at heel (or on the lead). As you walk, let the pup see you drop a dummy on the ground. Don't let the pup have it. Blow your whistle and say: 'leave it'. If he isn't quite steady, just grab him by the scruff of the neck or tread on the trailing lead to stop him making a dash for the dummy. Then you and the dog continue walking at heel as normal for a few yards. Now stop, turn round and hup the dog. Make sure he is pointing in the direction of the dummy, and can see it clearly on the ground. Tell him 'Snipe (or whatever his name is), get out!' and let him run off and fetch the dummy. Once he has picked up the dummy, encourage him to return quickly to you by blowing the return whistle. Insist on a proper delivery, even at this early stage. Ask the pup to come right up to and sit at your feet, then take the dummy from him very gently. Don't be rushing up to him and making a grab for the dummy, or yanking it out of his mouth as he comes flying past. Everything must be very calm and slow. And there's no need to go mad about praising him – too enthusiastic praising can break a youngster's concentration as well as overexciting him.

Do make sure that the youngster is on the whistle properly, and dispense with the lead as soon as possible. You will find that you can increase the difficulty of the exercise very rapidly. First of all, just walk further, so that the pup is 'getting out' (i.e. going back along the path) further and further. Also don't leave the dummy in very plain view. Hiding it won't make it much more difficult at all for a dog with a good nose. Always use somewhere like a path or lane with hedges on each side, so that the pup can only go in one direction – the right one! This will get him used to retrieving in the style that will be required as a trained dog, by going in long, straight lines in the direction of the retrieve. It also minimises the chances of the dimmer sort of dog failing to remember where the retrieve is. Dogs with good noses will dash immediately to the dummy in a straight line. I suspect that these dogs are actually following your foot (and his paw) scents on the ground leading the way back along where you have just walked. This is the same thing a good spaniel will do when it is following a runner. Later on when it comes to laying blind retrieves, do bear this in mind – you don't want to be simply repeating this early lesson.

Once the youngster is performing this first retrieving exercise confidently then you can start introducing all sorts of extra elements. Drop the dummy and carry on walking as before. Stop and hup the dog and drop a second dummy down. Then you and the dog walk back to the first dummy, hup the pup and then send him back for that second one! You can even introduce a third dummy. Send the dog for the first dummy and let him retrieve it. The drop another dummy and walk away from it, but don't send the dog until you have dropped a third dummy.

You can introduce all sorts of variations on this exercise. Get to the point where you can drop dummies in front and behind and send the dog for whichever one you want, in any combination you want. Remember, though, to use that straight line of a path or a fence, and make sure you have the dog pointing in the direction you want him to retrieve every time. Don't overdo things. You don't want the pup getting confused or uncertain or bored. I have always found they pick the lesson up very easily, and the temptation is to turn it into a party piece. Instead you should realise that this is just 'Retrieving 101' and you will be quickly ready to move on.

The next stage, still using this same exercise, is one of the first really crucial retrieving lessons your pup will learn. As you know, the underlying aim of dummy work is to simulate a shooting situation and teach the young dog to remain obedient and steady despite the temptations and distractions offered by real-life shooting. So this advanced form of the exercise requires you to throw a 'diversion' dummy (probably one of the few situations where you will end up actually throwing a dummy). Commence exercise one as normal, to the point where you have sent the pup to retrieve the dummy. While he is running out, throw another dummy to the side. It should be level with you and where the dog can obviously see the dummy landing. This is the 'diversion'. If the dog turns and starts going to the diversion, blow the stop whistle and hup him. Send him out for the original dummy, making it really clear with your hand and body language which dummy you want. If the dog disobeys the stop whistle and continues to go for the diversion dummy, you can run up and stop the dog physically. This is why you throw the diversion to your side, to give you the opportunity to get between the dog and the dummy if necessary. When the dog is performing the exercise reliably, gradually make it more difficult by throwing the diversion dummy nearer and nearer the dog.

For a pup that persists in ignoring the stop whistle and running-in, you are going to have to back-track in your training to your earlier basic obedience work. I'm afraid it is rather like a child being 'kept down' in school. At any stage in training, if the youngster is not picking things up easily, or if obedience is getting a bit de-railed, you must just go back to the previous level of training. Don't worry about it. You have loads of time. I'm happy to have a dog that takes two or even three years to train and then never puts a paw wrong for the next seven years in the field. Rather that, than one which whizzes through training in eighteen months and then proceeds to inflict many years of misery on me and my shooting friends.

I use a couple of little tricks with young pups to stop them getting into the habit of zooming off the moment you throw the dummy. Have a small dummy or a tennis ball in your pocket when you are with the pup. Every once in a while you can hup him, then let him watch you throw up the dummy in the air and catch it yourself. There's no need to overdo this, but it just gets him used to the idea that a dummy can be thrown without it being a signal for mayhem! A similar exercise is to hup the pup and then throw the dummy backwards over your head so that it lands behind you. Usually the pup is unsighted enough to think twice about running in, but if he's a hard-going little chap and still makes a spirited attempt to get the dummy, you are already between him and it, so it's easy to stop him – remembering to blow the stop whistle and hup him properly.

If all is going well with the basic retrieve, you can rapidly move on to introduce blind retrieves. People get very hung up about so-called 'blind' retrieves, and you would think their dog was Einstein when it picks a blind retrieve. We call it 'blind' because the dog is unsighted to the fall of the bird (or dummy) and therefore has been unable to 'mark' its landing place. But remember about a dog's sense of smell being so much more developed than our own? The vast majority of apparently 'blind' retrieves aren't blind to a dog at all, because he can smell them just as easily as if he could actually see them lying there. So he isn't Einstein at all (unless Einstein had a very good sense of smell). Never forget in your dog handling that a dog's primary sense is the sense of smell, unlike humans, who use sight more than anything. I can't stress enough how much your dog perceives the world around him through smell rather than vision. Understand this and you will become one of those great dog handlers who can predict what his dog will do before the dog has even made up his own mind.

What really makes a retrieve difficult for a dog is if he can't smell it, rather than when he can't see it. As trainers we often unintentionally give a dog a very difficult retrieve by leaving it in a place where its scent is baffled – either by other stronger scents, or by wind direction, or by a scent-killer such as water or even some chemicals (for example, recently limed or fertilised farmland). This is the reason why dogs so often fail to pick 'marked' retrieves lying in what, to humans, is plain view in a puddle. The water has destroyed the scent, and a dog will always take his nose's word for it over that of his eyes. This basic error is often made by fairly experienced gundog people. I was competing a dog in a retrieving test being held as part of a large county show. The area for the test was near the car park and had been walked over, picnicked on and generally trashed by all the show visitors. Many handlers were baffled by their dogs' poor performances. When my own dog brought me back a discarded chicken baguette instead of the dummy, I merely congratulated him on his hunter-gatherer abilities, put my lead on and went to find an ice cream.

So when you are laying your 'blind' retrieves, remember that at this stage we want them to be straightforward, and to encourage the dog to use his nose. The difficult 'nose-blind' retrieves we will save for a more experienced dog. For the first blind exercise use a small fenced paddock, the corner of a field or even a lawn. The area just needs to have a very defined corner made by fence, wall or bush. Before the lesson, hide a dummy in the corner. Using a corner is important because it limits the search area and makes it easier for the dog to find. You don't want to dent his confidence by him failing. With the dog, start walking along the fence line just as if you were going to do the first exercise. Then hup the dog at about the normal distance from where the dummy would be, point him in the direction of the dummy and tell him to 'get out'. This is all so similar to the basic exercise that he will go without even noticing that he hasn't seen you drop a dummy. When he reaches the corner, he will find the dummy, and you have completed your first blind retrieve without any fuss at all. Well done, but remember, it's not rocket science!

As these blind retrieves start becoming established you can move away from the fence line so the dog is approaching the dummy from lots of different angles – but at this stage always hide the dummy in the corner so it doesn't become too difficult to find. Leaving the dummy in the same spot all the time doesn't mean the retrieves will be identical, because you will be sending the dog from different places and distances. But he will remember where he found it last time and this will give him the confidence to get out quickly and directly. Later, when you are working in the shooting field, his confidence in you, stemming from these early training exercises, will be really helpful in encouraging him to go out well on long, difficult retrieves.

The other aspect of retrieving that novices can get quite anxious about is crossing obstacles during a retrieve. Again, it isn't that big a deal, especially if you introduce the idea of jumping and climbing to the pup right from its earliest walks. I have yet to meet the spaniel pup who isn't a born escape artist. If they can climb out of the whelping box before they can even walk properly, jumping the odd fence when they are fully grown isn't going to present much difficulty. So don't be in a hurry to lift even quite young puppies over obstacles; let them find their own way of scrambling over, under or through the wall, gate, or fence. When you are out on walks you can toss a tennis ball across any little streams or dry ditches you might find to get the dog used to crossing something during the retrieve. Don't be embarrassed to jump over walls and fences alongside or in front of your dog.

Begin obstacle retrieves with this exercise. Standing quite near a small wall or fence (not barbed wire), throw a dummy down on your side of the wall, allowing the dog to mark it. You and the dog then jump the obstacle, leaving the dummy behind you. Turn round and hup your dog. Then send him back on his own for the dummy, using your normal command for a retrieve. As your work becomes more advanced you can vary this exercise by stopping your dog at the obstacle briefly before sending him on and over it, or by making the retrieve a blind one. You can also increase your distance from the obstacle.

As all these different retrieving challenges start becoming fluent, you can move on to difficult retrieves where the young dog is going to need help from you in order to find the dummy. This is known as 'handling the dog on a retrieve' and causes more grief in shooting and trials situations than almost any other aspect of gundog work. So let's take it step by step. If the dog cannot find the dummy without your help – and you know where the dummy is – then you can direct him to the dummy by using a combination of whistle, verbal and hand signals. The very first problem that arises in this situation is this: the handler doesn't know where the dummy is any more than the dog does! Don't laugh, it could happen to you – and if you are honest with yourself it may already have done. Have you ever laid a retrieve for your dog, then lost sight of it yourself and been unable to remember which clump of grass it is hidden behind? Or when out shooting, have you watched a picker-up waving his dog into completely the wrong area looking for a pheasant? Mis-marking on the part of the handler is by far the most common cause of failed retrieves. So, if you are going to be giving your dog directions, do make absolutely sure you know where that dummy is.

The next issue is the handling itself. The most effective way to direct the dog is by hand signals. Most spaniels respond instinctively to a big, sweeping pointing gesture from the hand upraised position to either left or right, and they naturally move in the required direction. But – and you'd be surprised to know how big a but this is – the dog must first see the hand gesture before he can follow it. I know that seems every bit as obvious as remembering where the dummy is, but in the stress of the moment, novice handlers constantly repeat the mistake of not getting the dog sitting up looking at them before they give the hand signal. Even on field trials it can be amusing to watch some poor handler frantically waving and whistling while the dog goes on beavering about regardless. When you need to give directions, remain calm, clear and precise. Blow the stop whistle and raise your hand in the traffic-stopping salute as you did when originally teaching hup. The dog should stop instantly and sit up and look at you. If he doesn't, don't on any account proceed with giving a hand signal. Instead call him into you and realise that you have to take a step back to your earlier obedience lessons.

When the youngster is sat up looking at you (and not before!), very clearly and calmly move your hand out in a big arc from the raised position, directing towards the spot you want. Imagine a policeman directing the traffic, and keep the gesture big and unhurried. If your dog is uncertain, there are excercises you can do with dummies to help him get the message. Sit the dog up and let him see you drop a dummy to one side and another to the other. When you send him, he will instinctively want to go to the second dummy, but you can use body language and hand signs to send him to the first instead. This gives him the idea of going where you point.

Apart from going left or right, the other direction you will need to give your dog is to go further back, and with spaniels especially this can be problematic. It is quite a common fault – even on supposedly marked retrieves – for the spaniel to get about halfway to where you want him and then lose confidence and stop and look at you or even come back towards you. To get an idea of why this might be the case, just drop down on your hands and knees to get a dog's eye view of the terrain, you'll be surprised how different it looks. To teach your dog to go further back when you ask, use this exercise. Let your dog mark a retrieve and walk him away from the dummy as usual. Sit the dog up, but this time continue walking on a little way from him before you stop. Then send your dog back for the retrieve from where he is sitting. This will give him the idea of being handled even when you are some distance from him.

Whenever you are handling a dog, especially on a difficult retrieve, keep your verbal command as simple as possible. You will hear people using a combination of commands and even different sorts of whistles. Sometimes it sounds like a running commentary: 'get out, over, over, go back'. I can just about remember *The Golden Shot* on telly, and the whole thing can get very 'left a bit, right a bit, right a bit, fire'. To the dog, of course, it's completely meaningless. And in fact, if you listen carefully to nervous handlers in stressful retrieving situations, most of the time they are just babbling pretty much every command in their repertoire. Personally, I'm easily stressed, so I just use 'get out' coupled with the stop whistle and left/right hand signals. My dogs have learnt that 'get out' means go out in a straight line until either you find the retrieve or you hear the stop whistle. Once they hear the stop whistle, they stop and look at me, see which way my hand is moving and go that way. If I need them to go further back from the point at which I blew the whistle, I will make a throwing gesture from my raised hand and shout 'get out'. Anything more complex than that and I get confused, let alone the dog.

Try not to get hung up on very long distances at this stage, and don't go for the long ones all the time. Keep dropping back to shorter distances. This helps to build the dog's confidence, and it also prevents him from getting used to going out exactly the same distance every time. People who use dummy launchers a lot often end up with dogs who go out sixty metres and only sixty metres, because that is the range of a dummy launcher. Rather than having a set distance

There is no point giving the dog hand signals unless it is sat up looking at you ...

... then a clear hand signal stops the dog ready to receive directions ...

in mind, what you want to achieve is to be able to put your dog exactly where you want him – whether that is ten metres to the side but over a gully, or ninety metres out in front over open ground. If you can put your spaniel on a sixpence, your future retrieves in the shooting field are going to be easy money!

... the outstretched arm is easily seen by your dog ...

... and a clear hand and arm signal tells the dog to go to your right – the dog's left
(CHARLES SAINSBURY-PLAICE)

83

Make sure your dog delivers right in to your feet (CHARLES SAINSBURY-PLAICE)

Simon Tyers receives a perfect delivery (CHARLES SAINSBURY-PLAICE)

TROUBLE SHOOTING

I can't get my pup to fetch

Try not to worry too much about it. Make sure neither you nor anyone else in the family throws a young pup lots of retrieves. Remember the number of retrieves can build up. If everybody in a family of Mum, Dad and three children throws just ten retrieves a day for the youngster, that adds up to fifty retrieves in a single day – forty of which you may not know about, and far too many for any dog any day. Leave retrieving for a while. When you come back to it, use something that the pup is already interested in. I had one pup who did much of his early retrieving on pine cones! Never over-do dummy work with a sticky retriever, and don't be disheartened, they usually have a much better attitude to the real thing.

The pup picks up the retrieve fine, but then won't come back to me

This was exactly Pepper's little game when she was a young pup. She would show me the retrieve and then play-bow, hoping for a big game. In this situation, never be tempted to chase after the dog to get the dummy (and don't let your family anywhere near retrieving exercises). Definitely don't praise or plead with the pup in the hope that it will come. Instead, don't give the pup eye contact, just turn your back on it (while watching it out of the corner of your eye). Most pups will get uncertain at this point and come rushing to you with the retrieve. Turn round, drop down, and, praising the pup while the dummy is still in its mouth, take the retrieve. Some trainers advise running away from the pup to get it to chase you. But that's a great game as well – and surely the pup is now training you, not the other way round! For a really determinedly playful pup (like Pepper), set up your retrieves somewhere near where there is a hedge or similar to hide behind. When the pup is playing with the retrieve, slip into your hiding spot and watch the pup come looking for you.

The pup doesn't seem to want to carry the retrieve and keeps dropping it halfway back

Are your dummies brand new? For some unknown reason a few dogs don't like the feel of a new, very firmly stuffed dummy in their mouths. I had this problem with Ricky and got through it by using an old puppy-dummy or a rolled up sock. You can use anything that the pup likes carrying. Be careful also that a young dog isn't getting distracted. In your pleasure that he has found the dummy, don't start yelling your praise immediately as this can break his concentration or make him think the exercise is over. Instead just quietly pip

Jon Bailey prepares to give a hand signal on a retrieve (CHARLES SAINSBURY-PLAICE)

him back to you, then praise him while the dummy is still in his mouth before you take it from him.

My youngster won't get out in a straight line but just keeps hunting around the place

First be absolutely sure he knows he's being sent on a retrieve rather than just going hunting. Make sure your commands and body language are quite different. Sometimes a spaniel on a field trial will be sent to 'eye wipe' another competitor's retrieve before he's even had anything shot over him – this is a true test of whether the dog really understands what you want. If he knows he is retrieving and still messes around, go back to all those boring, straight-line dummy retrieves you did at the beginning – making sure to use quite a narrow and well-defined lane or path for the exercise.

6.
READY, STEADY, STEADINESS

If I ever get divorced it will be because of unsteadiness – not my unsteadiness, of course, or my husband's, or even the unsteadiness of our dogs. No, it will be the unsteadiness of other people's gundogs that eventually drives a wedge between me and my husband. My husband is a keen double-gun man who enjoys nothing more than a 1980s-style hot barrel blast on a commercial driven day. He's so focused on his shooting that he never notices the truly appalling standard of dog work on many of these shoots. The most common fault is pickers-up who can't stop their dogs running-in during the drive and retrieving birds that have fallen dead beside the Gun – the prerogative of the peg dog if ever there was. Bad as this is, it isn't the worst thing I've seen. On one shoot the manager's Doberman ran wild, mouthing birds and dropping them. Elsewhere I regularly see (and hear!) beaters' dogs chasing way too far in front of the beating line, flushing pheasants in the wrong direction, and even barking. At the worst dog-work shoot I have ever been on a beater's dog ran clean out of the cover during the drive, met a picker-up's dog coming from the opposite direction, and the two then proceeded to fight it out over a fallen bird. All this accompanied by incessant howling from a pup locked in the head keeper's truck!

My husband says none of this is important; that I am just a typical 'dog lady' stomping about in tweeds and pearls, bossing everyone around. And many who work their dogs wildly, on either large or small shoots, would agree, insisting that it's birds in the bag that count, rather than any of the niceties. The trouble is, the birds don't get in the bag. Either they are flushed unshootable, or the dogs fail to pick them, or they are pegged – and those that do end up in the bag are often inedible due to tearing and hard mouth. It is perfectly possible to have massive days, and, equally, small semi-driven days, without the quality of

dog work suffering. I particularly enjoy partridge days in the Midlands with pickers-up standing in the line alongside the Guns, all of us working together to enjoy great sport. Some enlightened gamekeepers even arrange their own training days during the summer for their beaters and pickers-up.

Good dog work, whether it is from your own dog or those around you, adds hugely to the pleasure of a day's sport, whether it's walked-up or driven, private or commercial. And regardless of the personal satisfaction it gives, I believe working a steady dog is a mark of respect to your quarry, your fellow Guns – and ultimately, yourself. The problem is that many who have come to the sport in the last decade or so have never really had the chance to experience excellent, steady dogs working. When was the last time you saw a proper peg dog sitting unflinchingly through the drive, without assistance from any form of slip-lead or dreaded screw, its noble gaze fixed devotedly on its master? Under these circumstances it isn't surprising that a lot of people who take dogs out shooting with them don't fully understand what steadiness is, or appreciate the massive difference it makes to the quality of your sport.

It is easy to confuse steadiness and obedience. So far with your training, all we have asked of the pup/young dog is that he be obedient to all your commands during the learning exercises. These exercises have all taken place in very controlled situations, engineered to make it as easy as possible for the pup to be obedient. So by now he is certainly stopping whenever you blow the whistle, and obeying all your commands 100 per cent of the time. Don't think that means he is steady! If he were to flush a pheasant or bolt a rabbit tomorrow, he would almost certainly chase it, no matter how hard you are blowing the whistle. A steady dog is one who 'drops' (sits still) to the flush/bolt of game; the sound of shot; and the fall of dead or wounded game. Moreover, a truly steady dog (of field trials standard), will do this automatically without any command from its handler. That is PhD level steadiness, and even on trials you will hear a nervous handler give a quick blast on the whistle, just to be on the safe side, when a particularly tempting rabbit bolts from the dog's nose. In a nutshell: obedience is what you get from a dog that hasn't been tempted; steadiness is what you get from a dog that has overcome temptation. Up until now in your training you have been doing everything you can to prevent your pup from going wrong. Now we are going to do almost the opposite, and start putting him into situations where he is likely to misbehave.

Opposite: *Jon Bailey's dog remains steady while waiting to be sent for a retrieve* (CHARLES SAINSBURY-PLAICE)

Of course, these situations will still be highly controlled by you, so that the transition from basic obedience to true steadiness 'under fire' will be smooth. The first precaution to take is to make sure your youngster is genuinely obedient to all commands, especially that he is 'on the whistle'. Here's a very simple test which will give you an accurate assessment of where your pup is on the curve of obedience to steadiness.

Find somewhere without a lot of distractions – I do this test with the pups on the lawn at home. Take your dog off the lead and walk it to heel. As you walk, blow the stop whistle. Normally we all have a tendency to stop and stand still ourselves when we have blown the whistle, and often it is that body language to which the dog is responding. So this time make sure you keep walking and make no other signal as you blow the stop whistle. The dog should stop and sit immediately, remaining where it is although you are continuing walking away from it. You would be surprised how many supposedly fully trained dogs fail this test. When Ian Openshaw is giving a master class to a group of dog handlers who are perhaps a little over-impressed with their abilities, he will get everyone doing this test – usually with the desired effect of bringing us down a peg!

If your pup does pass first time, congratulations, you've obviously worked very consistently on obedience. But the full test isn't over yet. Return to the dog, and, standing beside him, throw a stone into long grass about ten metres away from you. Let the dog get out as if to retrieve. He won't be able to find the stone, and while the dog is hunting about in the grass, blow the return whistle. Make no other signal. If the dog stops hunting and returns immediately this means he is genuinely obedient to your whistle commands. The test will show up any flaws in the three fundamentals of basic training: heeling, stopping and returning. It also highlights whether the dog is responding correctly to the whistle or has become dependent on your general body language and verbal commands.

If your dog doesn't achieve one or other of the three aspects: heeling, stopping and returning, don't regard it as a negative thing. All that has happened is that you have been given the opportunity to identify and correct any weaknesses in the dog's work very early on – before it has caused problems during the more advanced training.

For a lot of spaniels (especially Cockers), the first hurdle – heeling – is rather harder than sitting and returning. As we discussed in Chapter Two, heel-work is quite a controversial issue with spaniels, and your approach to it very much depends on what kind of working gundog you are aiming for. If you want the spaniel to be mainly a very steady dog to sit on your peg and generally be a nice

Wendy Openshaw's dog waits to be sent on a retrieve (CHARLES SAINSBURY-PLAICE)

family gundog, then heeling can be introduced gradually almost as soon as the very young pup goes on a collar and lead. But spaniel purists will tell you that too much heel-work too early, will produce a pottery kind of dog that is unwilling to leave your side in order to get on and hunt or even get out on a blind retrieve. Clearly this is not what you want for a dog that is going to go rough shooting or field trialling. In these specialisations, the dog spends most of its time either hunting, or retrieving, or on a slip-lead waiting to work, so heeling isn't particularly important.

All the youngsters I keep are trained with field trialling in mind. Even if they don't eventually make the grade, they will tend to become rough-shooting or all-round dogs. However I start the heeling work at pretty much the same time as I do the lead work, the only difference being how much I insist on it being paw perfect. To decide this you have to judge your pup's personality as well as its ultimate job. If he is the clingy type, without huge amounts of get-up-and-go, he will find heeling quite easy – but you shouldn't overdo it, because you need to encourage his independence a bit, and a lot of heel-work won't help that. Most of mine are quite hot, so heeling really goes against the grain. You will see this with many of the top trials dogs. Cockers are the worst, especially on the slip-lead. They constantly play with the lead and weave in and out of it, so that at trials (when you must have the dog on the lead between runs) you often end up just carrying the little swine as it's less irritating in the end!

So heeling isn't the be-all-and-end-all, but if your youngster isn't yet heeling well enough to take the test, then you need to put a bit of work in. Most trainers recommend just letting the slip-lead trail over the dog's back so that he thinks he's still on the lead. Cocker spaniel trainers know better. I don't know many spaniels (Springers included) that aren't bright enough to know instantly whether they are on or off the lead. Just to remind myself how futile this is, I tried it with Ginger and Pepper. First I taught them to heel nicely on the lead, without any pulling me about, so I could hold the lead draped over my fingers. Ginger tugged a bit at first, but soon got the message. Pepper was better, trotting along meekly at my side. Then I tried the lead-draping technique with Pepper – who instantly took off hunting into a deep, very muddy patch of cover (completely trashing the lead!).

Here's a method to overcome this. Use a collar and lead for this exercise instead of a slip-lead. Put the lead on as normal, but also loop a length of fishing line through the dog's collar. When you take the lead off, the dog won't be able to feel it is still attached to the fishing line, so it will come as a surprise when you are able to control him. Leave the line trailing, and as soon as the dog comes off heel, quickly tread on the line to bring him up short, while you firmly repeat the command 'heel'. If you are not too quick on your feet, you can just loop the line lightly over your hand and then jerk it up firmly as if you were indeed hooking into a fish. Work somewhere that has no distractions, like a narrow lane or driveway. The key thing is to surprise your young dog – so that he realises that even when he feels as if he is free, he is actually still under your control!

If I'm out walking a pup, I sometimes break off a very light, slender and long twig, or even a long blade of grass or ear of wheat. If the pup is putting his head too far in front I use my twig to tickle his nose or his backside. Obviously this isn't a punishment, but it has the desired effect of surprising him and getting his attention so that he remembers to concentrate on me all the time. Don't be tempted to use a flexi-lead – a long cord that is coiled into a spring release mechanism. Flexi-leads encourage the dog to pull against the lead, and they allow for it. Whenever you put the break on the release mechanism there is always a slight time lag before the dog feels the jerk. Flexibility, pulling, time lags before enforcing commands – all these things are disastrous when training a gundog. The lead's very name, 'flexi', tells you the problem. There is nothing 'flexi' about good obedience training. It is black or white, off or on. Whenever I go to the park and see people being dragged along by rude, ignorant dogs, the flexi-lead is part of the problem. Never, ever let your dog drag you on a lead.

If your dog has passed his obedience finals, then work with dropping to dummies and live game in the rabbit pen is not far off. But there is some extra practice you can do in controlled situations which will help to pre-steady him before he starts on the real thing. Would your young dog continue to sit patiently waiting for a command with you out of sight? Now is the time to find out. Sit him up. Leave him, and then hide. I often do this out walking. I can hide behind a hedge and watch the dog without him seeing me. But if you are not confident he will stay, start off at home. Get a friend whom the dog doesn't know very well to sit and watch the dog for you, while you go into the house – your friend can then signal you if the dog moves. I have been leaving Ginger outside the back door while I pop inside, and I'm glad to say he has waited very happily.

The dog's confidence in you is crucial for success in this exercise. When I first started training pups, I used to have more trouble with this lesson than any other. Most of the time the pups would be crawling after me, or getting upset when I left them, and once or twice a pup just strolled off elsewhere! But I haven't had any problems at all teaching it to Ricky, Ginger or Pepper. I believe this is because I finally know what I am doing when it comes to training, and my self-belief projects itself to the dogs. They know I'm confident, and that makes them more relaxed. They have learnt from the moment they could walk that I'm not going to let them get away with anything, but nor am I going to let them down. This kind of consistency is an absolute fundamental for successful dog training.

Another good preparation for your entry into the rabbit pen, and all its many distractions, is to take your youngster out and about a lot and do your obedience lessons in lots of unusual places. Everywhere from an empty pheasant release pen to the local game fair will help your pup learn that he can enjoy life, but still be obedient, no matter what excitements are on offer. If the game season

'What next, boss?' (CHARLES SAINSBURY-PLAICE)

has started, I will sometimes put the pup in the vehicle, with trained dogs, on our own shoot. The pup stays in the vehicle with an older dog when there is a drive on, and then pops out between drives to see people and experience smells. If I'm not shooting I will occasionally bring the pup out on a lead during a small drive and stand him a long way behind the line so he can hear the shots without them being too many or too loud. He can also get the idea that you just sit there and nothing too exciting happens. You have to be very careful not to get tempted to let him have a retrieve at this stage – it's far too soon.

At the same time as you are doing all this, you can now start asking for complete steadiness to the thrown dummy as it falls to the ground. Most of your dummy work up until now has been with dummies that are just dropped or hidden, which don't pose a temptation to the youngster to run in. Novice handlers who start off in the very early days by throwing lots of retrieves for their pups and letting them chase in after them often have problems at this stage because there is suddenly a big difference in what they are demanding. But if the pup has never been in the habit of running after a lot of thrown retrieves in the first place, it's unlikely he will start now when you test his steadiness to the fall of a dummy.

While he is out hunting, throw a dummy in the air to fall where the youngster can see it. If you have been thorough with the diversion exercises in Chapter Five, the dog should sit immediately and wait for a command. If he needs a little help, blow your stop whistle. But don't get into the habit of always blowing your stop whistle. You want the dog to stop automatically as he sees the dummy (either in the air or falling). As ever, if it doesn't go well, just drop back a stage for a day or two before trying the exercise again. Another quick revision lesson you can do is throwing the dummy behind you over your head to give you a chance to intervene if the dog makes to run in.

If he's obedient, you can start introducing the sound of a shot to go along with it. It's at this point in training where a lot of people get very hung up on equipment. They buy a starting pistol to make the shot sound, and while they are at the gun shop (or online), they see a dummy launcher and even a bolting rabbit kit. Although I have bought all these items in the past, I find I hardly ever use them now. For one thing, it is a lot of paraphernalia to remember to carry with you when you are popping out for a quick ten minutes training after work. And they all have drawbacks compared with the real thing. The starting pistol noise is surprisingly different from a shot gun, and some young dogs respond less well to it than the sound of a 28 or 20 bore shotgun. Gun shyness is not a common problem among modern spaniels, who tend to be brought up hearing plenty of louder noises than a gun! Dummy launchers can be quite tricky to handle, and also encourage the dog to be fixated on the launcher rather than the dummy. As for the bolting rabbit, I'm afraid mine is still in the box! By all means experiment with equipment, you can even get traps to release live pigeon, but personally I'm all for me, a whistle and a tennis ball.

While you are working on these last few pre-rabbit pen steadying exercises, make a plan for how you are going to go about your live game work. Those who live in urban areas without ready access to shoots, rabbit pens etc, will find the next chapter helpful. If you are lucky enough to have your own rabbit pen, that's great, but few novice amateur trainers have space for one. Usually a professional trainer or possibly gamekeeper is the contact. Gundog training clubs can be very helpful too. Contact the Kennel Club field trials department and they can give you a list of all the gundog training and field trialling societies in your area (See Appendix III).

This is a good time too, to remind yourself how you intend to use your dog when he is trained, and you may even have changed your opinion on this. Some people set out training their first spaniel with the idea that he's going to be mainly for picking-up/peg work, but get so excited by watching him hunt that they decide to get more involved in rough shooting. That's exactly what happened with me, and I'm so glad it did! It's so exciting shooting over spaniels, I wouldn't want anyone to miss out on it.

When you introduce live game, this is when you really start differentiating your training depending on your objective. Field triallers will head for the rabbit pen very early on with their seven- or eight-month-old pups, because ultimately style, pace and hunting drive are what you need to be successful in a trial. In a normal trial competition, the dog may have as few as four or five birds or rabbits shot over it. In terms of steadiness, you just need to be able to keep the dog steady for as long as that takes! But for a basic shooting dog, obedience and reliability over a full day's shooting (driven or rough) are more important, so the rabbit pen is used to reinforce obedience to commands more than to encourage hunting drive. With purely a peg dog, you need to emphasise the patience he will need to sit still through a long drive, so the youngster might do very little in the pen other than sit still and watch rabbits running around.

When you get into the pen, begin by walking the dog to heel as you wander around the pen. Pip the whistle and sit the dog up as usual. That is the first lesson – that nothing is done any differently just because the dog is in the pen. Walk towards a rabbit, and as the dog sees it, pip your whistle and make him sit up. All you want to achieve at this point is for the dog to continue to do exactly as it is told, despite the new exciting situation. Five minutes is long enough for a lesson. If anything goes wrong, just leave the pen and work again on getting the basics perfect for the next couple of days. If you have covered your basics properly you won't have any problems.

When this first experience has gone smoothly, don't keep repeating it, because you can move on now to some more demanding steadiness tests. With the dog heeling, walk him into a spot where he can wind a rabbit in its seat. Let the dog get near enough to the rabbit for it to get up and run away – a sort of slow motion bolt! As soon as the rabbit moves off its seat, pip your whistle and stop the dog. Repeat these lessons every day for a week and then give your dog a few days off so it can all sink in. When you go back into the rabbit pen, you can find out whether the dog is still going to be obedient, or whether he will hot up with his increasing confidence. Some youngsters are good as gold the first couple of times – but often it is only because they are so gobsmacked by it

Perfect steadiness in all situations (CHARLES SAINSBURY-PLAICE)

all! Once they have got used to the new situation, they may start playing you up a bit.

For many of us, this can be the first time when things start going wrong. A previously paw-perfect young dog, who clearly knows and usually obeys all the commands, suddenly turns into a hunting, chasing-obsessed fiend! The thorny question then is what to do next? Should we rush up to the dog, yelling curses, and proceed to swing him round our head by his ear? Mad as this may seem, I have actually seen it done in the past – and once upon a time something similar was the received wisdom for training hard-going spaniels. Ian Openshaw comments: 'It's with exercises like this that you get a lot of people charging in and giving the dog a thrashing for chasing. But if you genuinely have the dog on the whistle all you need to do is blow the stop whistle – and whose fault is it if the dog is not on the whistle? What you need to remember is that if a young dog does anything wrong, it is actually your fault because you have not trained it properly in the first place. One of the worst things is to get frustrated while you are training in the rabbit pen. A wrong move by you could put the dog off its work completely. So if anything starts going wrong, get out of the pen and sort it out later by going back to the basics.'

Think of it logically. The young dog goes in hard on a rabbit, bolts it off the end of his nose, and in the excitement of the moment, takes a few steps to chase the rabbit. At which point you descend like a tempest and give him the telling off of his young life. Don't be surprised if your youngster then becomes reluctant to enter cover and nose out a rabbit when necessary. Ultimately you want a spaniel who is going to ram his nose up the backside of a reluctant pheasant or lazy rabbit, not a young dog who dithers around the edge of cover wondering when you are going to start shouting again.

If the youngster is too hot at first, don't rush into thrashing mode. Simply blow the stop whistle. If he still doesn't stop, run up to him, grab him by the scruff of the neck, sit him up and blow the stop whistle. Then put the slip-lead on and leave the pen. Next lesson, test his steadiness by rolling a tennis ball past his nose or chucking a dummy in his path when he is hunting. Then back into the pen and repeat the early pen exercises before letting him have another go at bolting a rabbit. It is very likely that all will go well this time. If he is steady, walk up to him and praise him thoroughly before continuing with the lesson.

All young dogs know the difference between praise, reprimand and full-on punishment. If you are absolutely clear and consistent in praise and reprimand throughout your pup's training, you will rarely need to punish. To praise your pup, use a soft, warm tone of voice; give a gentle eye contact; and as long as your pup is not too over-excitable, a little physical stroke of the head and neck. To reprimand your pup, use a sharp, harsh tone of voice. I usually just say 'ach, ach'. Remove eye contact by looking over the top of the dog's head. When reprimanding, always start at the lowest level – you want to leave yourself somewhere to go if you do need to punish. For a full-on chastisement, I impose myself physically on the dog. I will run up to him, grab him by the loose skin under his chin and give him a good shaking, while telling him off. Sometimes, if he's been trying to get a bit dominant, I roll him over onto his back and stand over him. Watch how dogs assert themselves on each other. A top dog will often nip the nose of a younger dog who is being cheeky.

Over the years I have found that the worst punishment of all that I can give my dogs is to ignore them. The withdrawal of that precious link between them and the boss is upsetting for young dogs. This has made me realise how often people punish their dogs completely unwittingly. Out shooting I see people ignore their dogs all the time. They fail to chastise bad behaviour – but disastrously, they also fail to notice and reward good behaviour. The worst of all worlds is unfortunately all too common among inexperienced dog owners. Having been told they must be firm, they are quick to spot and punish bad behaviour, but then they don't notice and praise the dog when he is doing well. You then end up with a dog whose only interaction with his handler is to be chastised. Rather than not have any reaction at all, the dog quickly develops a pattern of seeking out punishment by behaving badly. The owner has turned him into a crime-junky because that's the only behaviour that gets the dog attention – 'reward' from the dog's point of view. Dogs like this, through no fault of their own, essentially become untrainable. So remember to be a positive reinforcer. Notice and reward good behaviour. Be firm but fair over deliberate naughtiness. Don't over-react to training problems by punishing when in fact you should merely re-teach the exercise.

TROUBLE SHOOTING

When I ask him to sit and stay, he always crawls towards me

Often an issue when the youngster is not very confident in you. Make sure your behaviour is always consistent, and do be especially aware if you have a tendency towards a sharp temper or moodiness. Sit the dog up and back off from him in a gradually widening spiral. Return to him and praise him. Gradually get further away until the point where you can briefly slip behind a hedge. Occasionally call him back to you, but most of the time you should return to him.

He won't stay, but dashes off

Blow the stop whistle. Walk quietly up to him and drag him back to where he was when you first asked him to stay. When you back off from him, make sure you hold eye contact and keep your hand up high in the stop signal as you walk. Do the exercise somewhere as boring as possible, and repeat it patiently until he gets the message.

My young dog barks occasionally when he is excited

There's no need to be particularly concerned about this, but be aware of it when you start introducing the more exciting retrieving and live game work. Always make sure that he's had a chance to run about and let off steam before you start doing a new lesson. He's probably an excitable type all round, so keep things quite calm and don't jazz him up by over-praising him.

My dog has chased and caught (pegged) a rabbit

These things do happen occasionally, and surprisingly often at field trials! It is usually a sign that you have a keen hard-hunting dog with a lot of drive. Beware of over-punishing – you don't want to put him off when the time comes to retrieve a rabbit that is only slightly wounded. Instead concentrate on your steadiness work and demand absolute whistle obedience. Next time you take him in the pen, be prepared. Work him with your whistle permanently in your mouth so that you are not fumbling for it if you need to blow the stop whistle urgently.

7.
DOG ABOUT TOWN

The good news about training and working an urban gundog is that it can be done! The bad news is that it is genuinely more difficult for town dwellers to have a working dog in their lives than it is for their country cousins. Throughout my career as a Fleet Street journalist, I didn't let myself have a dog; my working hours were too long. Many who live in the city or suburbs make the same decision – whether it's because of a stressful career, high-rise living, a hectic social life, or simply a busy road on the doorstep. But it is possible to train and work your spaniel from an urban backdrop, as long as you are not battling every one of those factors.

Do question yourself though. Does your job really allow the time needed not simply for training, but for the general welfare and care of a young spaniel? And it isn't only a matter of time. Urban lifestyles can be very stressful – are you going to be coming home in a bad mood too often to give your dog the consistent up-bringing it needs? What about family life? Is it a hectic household with both parents working, and children and teenagers coming and going at all hours? It will take a dog with an exceptionally good temperament to cope with all this, and spaniels are probably not the right breed. Finally, the environment is almost the most important of all factors. If you live right on a busy road or in a flat in the heart of the city, life is going to be uncomfortable and even dangerous for both you and your dog. Driving along a busy road on the outskirts of Bristol recently, I witnessed a terrible accident. A young woman pulled into the opening in front of a friend's house. Getting out of the 4x4 she walked round to the back of it and opened up. One of her dogs, a Doberman, jumped straight out of the vehicle into the path of an oncoming car. There was nothing the car driver, or anyone, could have done – except not to let the situation develop in the first place.

Don't let your dogs jump out of the vehicle until you are ready

In an urban environment, everyday life with your dog can flip into tragedy in seconds, after only a moment's lack of planning and concentration. If you want to make a success of your urban gundog, you are going to have to be very disciplined about it right from the outset. Your own personality will be very important. If you are a well-organised type, with a focused mindset, and you have honestly assessed the situation to be feasible – then by all means have a go, and this chapter will give you lots of help. But remember that there are other options which might work better for you. Many city high-flyers have their peg-dogs actually based with a country-dwelling friend and pick them up just for shooting weekends. It's not ideal, but better than nothing if you can afford it! For spaniel-lovers though, this is unlikely to be enough, as we want to be able to work and handle the dog in a variety of situations. Getting in touch with a professional handler can go some way to help out. You can build a great relationship with one of the top professionals. They are usually very flexible about training and working the dog and also getting you closely involved, even though you can't be full time. If this is your option, then start asking around at field trials or go online to see who might be able to help you out.

If you have decided you want to go solo, the single biggest rule you will need to follow is: discipline. And then some more discipline – not just the dog, but equally importantly, you. It is an absolute imperative that a city-dwelling dog must be 110 per cent obedient. A dog that won't obey whistle and voice commands instantly is a deal breaker when it comes to urban areas. And yet urban and suburban areas are crammed with dogs who don't obey their owners. This is because the owners don't have sufficient discipline themselves. In order to train a dog to be obedient and well disciplined, you yourself must be consistent, self-disciplined and well organised.

It is a sad fact that I have rarely seen an urban or suburban dog that I admire. Whenever I'm in a suburban park, or even in fields on the edge of the country-side, I am usually deeply concerned by the behaviour of the dogs being walked. I have seen a young yellow Labrador tugging the lead so hard that the child on the other end of the lead fell over the pavement and broke two front teeth. Urban dogs let off the lead in rural fringe areas are constantly chasing grazing ponies, deer and sheep. Any day in any park you can watch dogs running wild; snapping at other people's children and dogs; stealing things; knocking into push chairs; bowling up to very young children and putting their paws on the child's shoulders. What bothers me most is that nearly all these dogs are displaying overly-dominant behaviour.

All too often dogs with no structure or discipline in their lives end up maturing into dominant pack leaders who have the whole household singing to their tune. For those who are naturals with dogs and animals generally, especially country dwellers, this rarely becomes an issue. And of course lots of town dwellers do handle dogs very well – but the unavoidable truth is that more do not. It isn't just because the urban environment is different from the rural one. The whole lifestyle is different, and tends to encourage a mindset that isn't ideal for dog training. Life in urban households is often chaotic and unplanned – after all, with shops on the doorstep open round the clock, who needs to think ahead? For country folk, the nearest shop is often miles away, and usually closed, so you get used to planning at least some aspects of your life in advance. There is also a greater likelihood that country dwellers have been brought up with animals, and understand that a certain amount of regularity is needed for basic animal welfare. Your dog can't just pop out and buy himself a curry if he's hungry and there's no one about – but he will end up helping itself to take-away, which in the suburbs could easily be the next-door neighbour's pet rabbit!

So from the moment you get your pup back to your home in town, start thinking about structure and organisation. Because of space and neighbour issues, it is comparatively rare for an urban dog to be kennelled outside. Town dogs are, almost by definition, indoors dogs – whereas most country dogs live either completely outside in kennels, or live in a utility area within the house. Dominance is a much more important issue for an indoors dog than a kennelled dog – you don't want to find yourself with a young canine thug growing up surrounded by children and stressed-out adults. Be clear to yourself and your family that the pup is not going to be allowed to dominate the household. Make sure the dog has its own bed. Better still, an indoor pen works well in a busy urban home, as it becomes a refuge for the dog as well as keeping him out of trouble. In a dog's world being on top means being on top physically. There are lots of opportunities in the home for a dog to get on top by jumping on to chairs, tables, sofas. With big spaniels this is obviously invasive, but it is a mistake to think smaller breeds like Cockers can be allowed to get away with it. An ankle-biter at head height can cause serious facial damage and disfigurement. A dog in the wrong place should be removed immediately and reprimanded if necessary.

Obviously urban dogs should never be left alone in the house while you are out at work, but don't fall into the trap of giving your dog the run of the garden while you are away. Intelligent gundogs left to roam will get into mischief. They will escape from even the most Houdini-proof garden, dig holes, chase squirrels, learn to bark – sometimes they may even be stolen. Where possible use a proper outdoor kennel with a small run. A gundog in full training and exercise doesn't need more freedom than this. Twice a day – in practice morning and evening, give your dog a good half hour of mixed training, and exercise. In many cases this will be more quality time with you than a rural dog would get with his owner. If you are going to be away all day, ensure there is someone to check on the dog. Don't let people pressurise you that 'the dog is being shut in a kennel'. A dog receiving the stimulation of regular training is quite happy to relax in his kennel with a bone.

Establishing routine and discipline at home will be a huge help to you in achieving the level of obedience you need to be able to train and exercise your dog in a busy urban environment. The most important thing is that you must be able to stop and sit your dog instantly on the whistle wherever he is. That's all there is to it. Get that right and you can train him on Hyde Park Corner without turning a hair. But if the slightest bit of ill-discipline creeps in (and it will usually be from you, not the dog), then life is rapidly going to become difficult. If you can sit your dog on command, then you can stop him running into the road, chasing animals, jumping up at children and generally getting into trouble. If you can't stop him, he'll end up spending his life on a lead, which is a far sadder outcome for him than having to cope with a little discipline.

Urban dogs don't get exposed to so many different animals as working dogs in the country, which means they can have a tendency to chase stock. When people ask how to stop their dogs from chasing sheep or cattle, the principle is just the same as it is for steadiness to game. You blow your stop whistle. If your dog is disobeying the whistle, then he can't be allowed near stock again until basic training is back on course. For the urban puppy you need to get the stop whistle fully established in the garden at home (or even indoors if you don't have a garden) before you venture into the park. Once you are out in public open areas, continue to spend time getting whistle obedience absolutely 100 per cent, just as described in previous chapters. There are many more distractions for a town dog, so it will require more patience and self-discipline from you both. But establishing this rule is fundamental to all your future gundog work in the town or country. The bonus is that if you can stop your dog instantly in a busy park, obedience on a shooting day will be easy.

Now you are sure your dog is steady, you can go on to use any number of urban open spaces for basic hunting, retrieving and steadiness training. There are stories of top professional handlers who teach their dogs steadiness using seagulls on the beach or pigeons in the square. Spaniel trainers have even been known to work their dogs on squirrels, bolting them up trees. I know of one trainer who takes his young dogs to a local leisure lake where the shore is heaving with semi-tame wildfowl, and this makes a great steadiness exercise. But it pays to remember that the general public won't have any idea what you are doing, and may not take too kindly to it! Out exercising, one of my spaniels retrieved a wounded duck from the next field – but it turned out there were picnickers there, whose child had just been feeding the duck. Things nearly got quite nasty!

Beware of using golf courses as training venues, no matter how tempting the cover in the rough, as golfers seem to have a poor sense of humour when their balls are retrieved from a position near the hole. While your dog is still inexperienced, use quiet times such as early mornings or late evenings. A suburban-dwelling amateur trainer, who has recently been having great success with his Flat-coated retriever in working tests, confessed to me that he trains his dog in the local park after dark, adding: 'He's had to get very good at blind retrieves'. You can use all sorts of open spaces imaginatively. A footpath between houses or even a canal towpath makes an excellent corridor for teaching your dog to go back in straight lines on blind retrieves. Suburban laurel bushes are great cover. Just steer clear of municipal flower beds when there's a park keeper around!

Many of the unexpected pitfalls that await all dog handlers are much more likely to occur in town or especially urban-fringe situations. Out in parks you do need to be cautious about other dogs. It is a fact of life that you are likely to meet untrained, aggressive, un-inoculated and stray dogs in these environments. So even if your dog is beautifully behaved, keep him away from strange dogs. Also watch your dog's every move really closely, even when you are not specifically training – outdoor urban spaces are restricted and town life is unpredictable.

Another growing problem for those living in semi-rural, suburban areas is the increase in dog theft. Dogs are being stolen from gardens, outdoor runs, and even while out on exercise or work. I once arrived on the scene just in time to prevent my young spaniel being loaded into the back of a passing people carrier. The driver assured me he thought the dog had strayed and was taking him to the RSPCA. But he hadn't let the dog 'stray' for very long, since he was in the middle of hunting a hedgerow, with me standing on the other side of the hedge! It is a criminal offence not to report the finding of a stray dog. All found dogs are deemed stolen unless their finding is reported to the police or the local authority dog warden, and these are the people to contact first if your dog has gone missing.

In large anonymous towns, it is easy for dogs to disappear into a 'stolen to order chain', whereas in the country you at least have some protection via the local community grapevine. So do take precautions (which I would recommend to both town and country dwellers). Have your dog micro-chipped by your vet, who will register you with The Kennel Club's Petlog scheme (See Appendix III). Keep all your dog's paperwork together in one place where you can lay your hand on it quickly. Include the dog's registration certificates, docking certificate etc and a recent photograph, together with a list of contact phone numbers including Petlog, local dog warden (See Appendix III), the police, local vets and rescue centres, gundog training clubs, dog breeders and pet shops. Do this now, so that if the worst happens it will enable you to react fast – which hugely improves your chance of recovering the dog. Use a collar stating that your dog is chipped (legally you should also add your name and postcode). Never let your dog roam alone at home or in the field (obviously gundogs don't do this anyway). Help reduce dog theft by never buying a dog or puppy without all of the correct paperwork. Also encourage your vet to scan all dogs routinely. Visit the Dog Theft Action website (See Appendix III).

The author with Gournaycourt Lemon

While we are on the subject of dogs and crime, it is important to realise that nowadays there is a huge amount of legislation regarding dogs. There are currently ten major Acts of Parliament affecting dog owners, not including local bye-laws. Most of these Acts are primarily concerned with the behaviour and welfare of dogs (pet dogs) living in urban areas. They haven't been well thought through in relation to working dogs, yet working dogs are rarely specifically

109

excluded from the legal requirements. This often means that owners of gundogs can unknowingly contravene the law in the course of normal training and working of the dog. This is especially the case for those trying to train a spaniel in an urban area, where there is little understanding of gundog work. Most of the time common sense will prevail, but where country sports are under pressure from antis, or there is a 'busybody culture', the letter of the law can be exploited to use against working dogs. In towns people are living much closer together and there is often a lot more active enforcement, which all adds up to urban gundog handlers having to be whiter-than-white relating to the law.

As you have recently bought, or are planning to buy, a spaniel puppy, you should be aware of an important piece of recent legislation relating to the docking of working dogs' tails. The Animal Welfare Act 2006 introduced wide-ranging provisions against neglect, cruelty, dog fighting etc, but the most important for shooting folk relates to tail docking in England and Wales (not Scotland). There is now an official exemption allowing tails of spaniels, HPR breeds and terriers to be docked legally by a vet as long as the requirements for proof of a working career are met. If you buy a puppy with a docked tail, make sure the breeder gives you the correct paperwork, usually a certificate from the vet. Remember too, that the Act obliges you to have your docked spaniel micro-chipped so that he can be matched up with his docking certificate.

One really important law relating to urban gundog handlers especially is the Clean Neighbourhoods and Environment Act 2005. Although it doesn't sound as if it has anything to do with dogs, this poorly constructed piece of legislation provides for a range of dog control orders, largely left to local authorities to enforce. There are fairly obvious regulations concerning dog fouling; allowing a dog somewhere it is not permitted (eg a children's playground); and keeping it on a lead where directed. But there are also provisions about the number of dogs that can be walked at one time, and even about when you can take your dog off the lead. We shooting folk often have to take several dogs out together; especially for training, when we might have half a dozen spaniels with us, but do this training in a public area such as a park, common or even moorland, and we could be breaking the law and fined £1,000.

Another scary piece of legislation is the Control of Dogs Order 1992, at the time a knee-jerk reaction to problems with pit-bull and mastiff-type urban dogs. This little-understood law states that any dog in a public place must wear a collar carrying its owner's name, address and postcode. Since gundogs rarely wear collars this law is broken on a daily basis by almost everyone who takes part in country sports. It is legal for your dog to be collarless 'while being used for sporting purposes' but how far that exemption extends can be hard to determine – for urban gundog handlers, the key question is: would that cover training? So get your dog a proper, legally tagged collar. Even if he doesn't wear it very often, you should have it to hand just in case.

The law that everybody knows about is the Dogs (Protection of Livestock) Act 1953. This is the famous piece of legislation which gives livestock owners the right to shoot dogs that are harassing their animals. But urban gundog handlers should remember particularly that this applies to absolutely any domestic livestock. It's not just farm animals but pets too, like guinea pigs, pet rabbits, horses, poultry – even next door's budgie! Other laws affecting your dog include the Breeding and Sale of Dogs (Welfare) Act 1999; Dangerous Dogs Act 1991; Road Traffic Act 1968; Animals Act 1971; Animal Boarding Establishments Act 1963; Dogs Act 1871. The Kennel Club does an excellent leaflet explaining all this, and if you have a neighbour who is a bit of a jobsworth, I would recommend having a copy handy!

TROUBLE SHOOTING

Our puppy is chewing everything

The obvious answer is, only because you are letting it! Never let him have the run of the house, and don't leave him to roam 'home alone'. Give him plenty of short training sessions, play and exercise. Then when you are not around, he goes into his indoor pen together with a proper dog chew and his favourite toys. Make arrangements for someone else to check on him if you have to be out for any length of time.

I'm ready to move on to training on live game but can't find any facilities

This is the most difficult obstacle urban gundog trainers face, especially novices. It is well worth considering sending the young dog to a professional for an eight-week stint of training at this point. He will have all the right facilities to bring your youngster safely through this crucial stage. It will also be a great way for the urban novice to make contacts that will be useful from now onwards.

Our local park is so full of dog walkers my dog is constantly distracted

Try training sessions very early in the morning or late in the evening, there will usually be enough light for you to see. You can also put the dog in your vehicle and take him to a less busy open space, perhaps a common or a larger park on the edge of your town. Your dog will need to get used to travelling to shoots in any case; this is a good exercise in lots of ways.

111

My neighbour is complaining about our puppy
A common problem for those living in densely populated areas. Don't leave the puppy out in the garden where it can get into barking competitions with other local dogs. Visit your neighbour (armed with a box of chocs or bottle of wine) and explain that you are in the process of training the pup. See if you can get the neighbour involved, or at any rate on your side – but if he is the complaining kind of neighbour, you will have to accept that this might be a long-term problem. Also ask yourself honestly if this is just the latest in a long line of issues between you and your neighbour, in which case it isn't really about the dog.

8.
PUTTING IT ALL TOGETHER

There is no doubt about it, basic obedience and early steadiness training can be a bit of a grind. I once asked a spaniel training friend why you see so few gundogs working that are genuinely on the whistle and steady. He replied: 'That's simple, it's because basic training is so bloody boring.' But if your training programme has been going steadily, at a slightly less tedious pace than watching paint dry, the moment has finally arrived when it starts getting exciting. The day you and your spaniel put it all together for the first time is guaranteed to be memorable. Over the years I have shot almost everything, almost everywhere – from thousand-bird driven pheasant days to lions in the Matetsi – but few sporting experiences are more rewarding than shooting a single grouse, or even just a humble bunny, over your own spaniel, trained and worked personally, by you.

Imagine the moment. It's a glorious day in late August, somewhere up in the Highlands. You and your young spaniel are working a gorsy bank. He's hunting beautifully – a nice, tight, flowing pattern, never too far away from you and missing no ground, just as you have taught him. He dives under a gorse bush, tail a blur, then freezes for a split second. You can tell by his body language that he is about to bolt a rabbit. It's sitting tight, but your spaniel shoves his nose up its bum, and the bunny's away – darting almost over your feet – while the dog sits like a rock, watching the bunny go. With the rabbit so near, you have plenty of time to get your 20 bore into your shoulder and fire, rolling the bunny over with the first barrel. You watch it lie there in case it needs a second shot, but no, one kick and it's dead. You open your gun and look to your dog, who looks back at you, just waiting for that command. You could tell him to leave the dead rabbit and go and pick it yourself, but since he's sat so well, the

Blue roan Field Spaniel dog Sidney (Cherryl D Smith)

dog deserves the reward of a retrieve this time. So you tell him, 'Get out' and before you know it he's back sitting at your feet offering you the rabbit. You take the rabbit, pop it in your game bag, and praise the dog. Job done, we'll eat tonight! The sense of camaraderie with your dog, and of self-sufficiency that this great sporting action has not involved huge teams of beaters and pickers-up (or indeed financial outlay) really does it for me, and I'm sure it will for you.

At this stage in training, we are getting very close to that moment. Most of the exercises in this chapter will be simulating it, and practising it in controlled circumstances. But don't rush to get to this point, and certainly don't commence this level of training just because your dog is eight months old or ten months old or even a year old. The guinea-pups, Ginger, Pepper and Ricky, are all there-or-thereabouts, but their learning curves have been quite different.

Ginger and Pepper are both eight months old now. Ginger has been exceptionally straightforward to train. You give him the lesson as described. He does it. He continues to do it from then onwards – he's a gundog writer's dream! My own rabbit pen is too small for a dog of his natural ability to learn much in, so he's gone up to Jon Bailey in Derbyshire, where he is already beginning to put it all together. Ginger's litter sister, Pepper, is rather different. Right from the start she has shown flashes of brilliance in both hunting and retrieving, but like her mother and grandmother, she is a bitch with her own agenda. It is very likely that once she starts working with 'the real thing' – game, she will start ignoring dummies. So although she would easily manage the next stage, I want to continue to do more challenging and demanding exercises while still using dummies.

Ricky, the Springer, is different again from the two Cockers. He is eleven months old, but I have only just started introducing him to the rabbit pen and live game. Ricky's strong point is his fantastic scenting ability, but he has poor concentration and is definitely a bit immature for his age. Training him so far has sometimes been rather frustrating. I can teach him an exercise in the fields at home, but when I try to repeat the lesson in a new environment, Ricky is away with the fairies! So I have spent the last three weeks deliberately taking him out and about to unusual places for his training. Once I am happy that he is consistently focused on me, no matter what the other stimulations he is experiencing, then I will continue with the work described in this chapter. But if he is still too goofy to progress, I will be patient and wait until he is genuinely ready, no matter what his actual age is.

Just as we gave your spaniel a key stage test before moving on to early steadiness and the introduction of the rabbit pen, so this time you need to review his progress again before proceeding to advanced work in the rabbit pen and then the shooting field. You need to assess your spaniel's level in all the four components: hunting, retrieving, flushing, and steadiness. To evaluate his hunting, take him to some light cover with plenty of game scent, but no actual game. Tell him 'get on' and watch his hunting. It won't be perfect, but he should be hunting close to you, making most of his turns without you needing to pip the whistle, and he should be covering all his ground. While he is hunting, hide a blind retrieve. When he is some way from it, sit him up and send him for the retrieve. When he brings it back, start hunting again. This time roll a tennis ball past his nose, or throw a dummy in the air, at the same time as making a noise. Hopefully you won't have to blow the stop whistle, but one pip is acceptable to be sure he stops and sits up immediately. All these tests simulate

115

the situations your young dog will encounter in the field. If he passes with flying colours, go into the rabbit pen and repeat the exercises you did in Chapter Six, testing his steadiness on sighting and gently moving a rabbit. If your youngster is still paw perfect, you are ready to go on and put it all together, first in the pen, but soon in the shooting field as well.

You can now start doing retrieves in the rabbit pen. A simple exercise is to drop a dummy in one corner of the pen. Then work the dog away from that corner until he flushes a rabbit. If the rabbit runs on ahead, tell the dog to leave it. Then call him to you and send him back out for the dummy. Stop the dog halfway and then tell him 'get out' and let him go all the way and bring back the retrieve. If the rabbit flushes back towards the dummy, don't send your dog on the retrieve because he will end up following the rabbit, which might encourage him to chase. Just pick the dummy up and repeat the exercise when the rabbit bolts the right way.

If your spaniel is going to be used mainly for picking-up or as a peg dog, he will need to be able to concentrate on just one bird at a time, even when there may be a lot going on around him. This isn't quite so important for a rough-shooting spaniel, as there tends not to be so much game being shot at one time. But teaching a spaniel to ignore diversions is helpful in all his work in the field. A useful exercise is to walk the dog at heel until you find a rabbit. Then roll a tennis ball past the rabbit and send your dog to retrieve it. If he tries to go for the rabbit, just blow your whistle to stop him, then firmly send him back for the tennis ball. This is quite an advanced exercise, so be patient, and very clear with your commands. If your youngster hasn't got it right or halfway right by the second or third time, leave it for another day. This exercise really shows up whether the dog is genuinely working for you, or more for himself. A youngster can give the appearance of doing pretty well, but when something a bit different or complicated is introduced, you discover he's just been on auto-pilot. This is exactly the sort of exercise I am using with Ricky to find him out. Ginger finds it all much easier. He is so well within his comfort zone in his lessons that he has plenty of brain-power left over to be aware of anything slightly unusual that I might be wanting him to do.

Apart from steadiness and retrieving, hunting is the other major aspect of a dog's work that you can work on in the rabbit pen. Bear in mind though, that good hunting dogs are born and not made. If your youngster is bred on field trial lines, with a lot of champions in his pedigree, it will certainly improve your chances of him being a good hunter with bags of style and drive. But there is a flip side to this. Hard-going hunting dogs can be rather hot to handle! Especially if you are a novice, you might not want to be trying to control a Ferrari of a spaniel every time you go out. I suffered with this a lot when I first began in spaniels. Luckily for me, my Gournaycourt line throws up a lot of really fast hunters, but it does mean you have to be totally switched on every time you go out. There are occasions when I think it would be nice to go out for a potter with a nice, ploddy hunter (though I know I would get bored). If your youngster turns out to be a Ferrari, fantastic, but don't end up wrapped round a hedge! Equally, if he's a bit more slow and steady, don't be constantly trying to rev him up. The plus side is that he's easier to handle. Just make sure he's thorough and not lazy in his work, and you will do very well.

With hunting, all you are looking to do in the pen is add a little polish. To start a young spaniel off hunting, let it find a rabbit. It will probably lose it, or you can stop the dog until the rabbit is in cover again. Then let the spaniel hunt on instinctively, looking for another rabbit. This is when you will see its natural hunting ability. The best will have drive and determination, with athleticism and speed in their work. Make sure your pen has varied kinds of cover. Mine has everything from nasty brambles to nice rhododendron bushes. The controlled circumstances of a pen make it a good place to allow the dog to work deeper cover. To encourage the dog to enter cover, you can use a dummy. Throw the dummy in with the dog looking. Then stand between him and the dummy so he is unsighted, and secretly pick up the dummy. Then ask the dog to hunt, using your 'get on' phrase. He will go in keenly, thinking the dummy is still there. Be careful though, not to let him think it is a retrieve, because he will lose confidence in you through not finding anything – so don't use your 'get out' phrase.

If all your early obedience and steadiness work has been really thorough, you should find that the rabbit pen phase goes very smoothly. Many trainers find that their dogs are ready to get out into the shooting field quite soon after they start in the pen. Once your dog is doing everything right in the pen, you can start on game outside the pen. If it is the right time of year, dogging-in recently released pheasants makes a great exercise for a youngster's first trip into the field. Hopefully your gundog contacts will be getting well established now, so you should be able to find a keeper who will allow you to do some dogging-in for him. Dogging-in is a very simple exercise, basically just what you were doing with rabbits in the pen, only with pheasants that flush instead of bolt. Be careful though, because young poults which aren't strong don't always take off very quickly, and the last thing you want is for your dog to peg one. Start by walking your dog to heel and kicking up the pheasant yourself, while the dog sits and

117

A low hand signal tells the dog which bit of cover to hunt (CHARLES SAINSBURY-PLAICE)

watches. When you are convinced of his steadiness, you can hunt him onto a poult. Give him a few retrieves with dummies while you are working, just to reward him for his steadiness. You may find he's so fixated on the bird, that even a retrieve thrown in plain view becomes like a blind – hence all your exercises in the rabbit pen! Be careful to keep a strong hunting dog working very close to you. Some of mine flush birds so hard that they fly clean over the release pen and we are back to square one. FTCh Kelmscott Whizz (Lynn) was such a clever Cocker that she would flush a bird with differing degrees of 'oomph' guaranteeing it landed in the pen!

Keep on with your rabbit pen work in between dogging-in days, and if all goes well, your spaniel is now ready to have his first experiences of being shot over. It's at this stage that you really do need a training assistant, especially to be doing the shooting. A lot of us press-gang family or friends into this task. Personally, I don't find this an ideal situation. I was training a youngster a while ago through horrid spiky cover with almost no game. After some really brave work, the young Cocker managed to show a little flush of three pheasants, who flew at a nice shootable height and distance out of the cover directly over my husband's head, where he made absolutely no attempt whatsoever to fire at them. The Cocker and I stood staring at him for a while with expressions respectively of bafflement and fury on our faces. I then intimated to my husband that those were exactly the kind of birds I was looking to get shot over the young dog. 'Oh, sorry about that,' came the casual reply, 'I didn't see them till too late, I didn't think there would be anything in there so I was thinking about something else.' Which is why it is a good idea to get hooked up with some other local gundog trainers who understand your point of view.

Not only will the local gundog club know where your nearest rabbit pen is, they will also offer training sessions, general advice, and invaluable access to the local gundog network. The Kennel Club has contact details of all the gundog training and trialling clubs in the UK, call and ask for the Field Trial department, or visit the website (See Appendix III). This is also the perfect time for you and your dog to get a couple of sessions in with a professional trainer. Don't ever think of this as a failure on your part. The most successful spaniel trainers in the country, both professional and amateur, all train together as often as they can fit it in. My own first experience of top quality dog work came this way. After a morning spent running unsuccessfully in a rabbit trial, I was invited to join my fellow competitors out on the hill training. Advice and tips were exchanged by everyone – though sadly I didn't have much to offer in return for all the great help I was getting. What a wonderful sport we are part of, where competitors in the morning become team-mates in the afternoon. To find professional trainers go to the websites shown in Appendix III. If you bought your puppy from a professional, keep in touch as they are usually pleased to help with training tips and info. Cocker championship winner twice-running, Simon Tyers, runs real shoot dog-training days in the Midlands. They are always heavily over-subscribed, but visit his website given in Appendix III for more information.

Once you have found your assistant you can start adding the shot into your work. As described in previous chapters, your young dog will certainly have heard a few shots by now. Go out training as normal, with your friend and a 20 or 28 bore. Have your friend standing at quite a distance from you and the dog, and start your dog off hunting through light, game-free cover. Throw a dummy in the air, and have your friend 'shoot' the dummy, while you blow the stop whistle and sit the dog up as usual. Most spaniels will sit instantly, perhaps quivering with excitement. On this occasion go and get the dummy yourself. Start the dog off hunting again and this time have your friend walking about ten or fifteen metres from you and the dog. Don't throw a dummy this time, but get your friend to shoot in the air. This simulates the frequent shooting situation of a gun shooting game which hasn't been found by the spaniel himself. A lot of spaniels drop to shot instinctively (even dear, dizzy Ricky!), but if he shows any signs of creeping, just blow the stop whistle.

From now on, you can continue with all your rabbit pen and retrieving exercises as normal, but just add the shot in most of the time. Once you are sure the dog is reacting well and not becoming unsteady, you will be able to be the one firing the shot yourself – but for the first couple of lessons, it does make life a lot easier if you have someone else to do it for you. I have always found that adding in the shot to the equation is one of the easier aspects of spaniel training. It is very rare for modern working-bred spaniels to be gun shy or even gun nervous. So far I haven't come across one. In the past a lot of young spaniels spent most of their time in a kennel, with little noise or stimulation of any kind. But one advantage of so many dogs being part of busy households is that they get used to all kinds of noises very early on, from frying pans clattering to the floor to the full rock concert experience!

This is a good time to practise doing some long and difficult retrieves, as the added encouragement of hearing a shot seems to give the youngster the incentive needed to commit to a retrieve that may take a bit of work to find. For these retrieves remember to get you or your assistant to fire in the direction of the retrieve. Distance in itself shouldn't be a problem if your basic training is right. All those early weeks of sending the youngster further and further back along the path for the dummy that he saw you lay should pay dividends now. But most experienced dog handlers would agree that one of the really difficult retrieves is where the dog has to leave the piece of cover it is working and go out some distance into bare ground to retrieve the fallen game. We all practise this a lot when we are out shooting with our dogs. With this kind of retrieve it is more important than ever to keep your command simple. You don't want the dog to have to remember anything complicated – Cockers, for example, would rather continue to hunt an inviting piece of cover, so it's best not to give them any excuse for being confused.

Perfect steadiness to the flush (CHARLES SAINSBURY-PLAICE)

Your dog may not leave the cover easily. When he gets out on to the bare ground he will almost certainly want to pull back into the cover. Stop him and tell him clearly what to do. The first time you introduce this advanced retrieve, show your youngster what is going on. Drop the dummy outside the cover or the wood or even a field edge and make sure the dog has marked it. Now go back into the cover with him and walk on a little way, before stopping him and sending him back. As you proceed with this, having a friend with you to shoot is really helpful. Ask him to walk along outside the cover, and then fire a shot at the retrieve you laid. This will really help your dog get the hang of it, and make him ready to leave cover easily in future. If you do want to have a go at

121

Tell the dog to 'get out' on the retrieve and indicate with your hand
(CHARLES SAINSBURY-PLAICE)

trialling, this is a really useful exercise because so many dogs get put out of the competition on this type of retrieve that being good at it can be a trial-winner for you. When you start rabbiting you will notice you often get a situation where the rabbit bolts from the cover and is eventually shot out on the bare ground at the edge. Because the rabbit will have left a good ground scent the dog will naturally go back and out of the cover for the retrieve, whether it is marked or not – unlike with pheasants.

With the addition of the gunshot, your simulation of every aspect of work in the shooting field is almost complete. But before you actually set off shooting, you need to check your spaniel will actually retrieve the real thing! I have noticed that Labrador trainers, concentrating almost completely on retrieving work, get quite excited about what is called 'cold game'. I think this is partly because a purely retrieving dog spends all his time retrieving game which he has not flushed himself. Spaniels, especially those used mainly for rough shooting, will mostly be retrieving game which they have found, flushed and usually seen shot. It seems pretty obvious to me that any dog so closely involved in the whole operation will be very keen on bringing back the end product – and this is usually the case!

Even so, you do need to do some practice. My spaniels are brought up retrieving everything from proper canvas dummies, to socks, to tennis balls, even an old running shoe! I introduce a rabbit skin dummy fairly early on, but if you haven't done so yet, now is the time. During the shooting season reserve a few brace of birds and put them in the freezer. You can go out with a .22 rifle and shoot a rabbit or two at any time. Because he is used to the rabbit skin dummy, your youngster should be pretty good with a cold rabbit. If you have the chance, try him with a freshly shot one that is still warm. He may play about with it a bit, but just encourage him to bring it to you and that should make his mind up. There will be plenty of opportunities to try him on all sorts of different rabbit retrieves when you first take him rough shooting.

Sending your dog on a retrieve away from the cover can be difficult – Ian Openshaw is successful with his dog (CHARLES SAINSBURY-PLAICE)

Dai Ormond gives his spaniel a long-distance command (CHARLES SAINSBURY-PLAICE)

Some youngsters are a bit put off by pheasants at first, and find the feathers rather confusing – but it's rare for them not to get the hang of it quite quickly. If your dog is showing a tendency to mouth the birds or tear at the feathers, put the bird in an old pair of tights. This makes the bird much more like a dummy and gives the dog a better idea of picking it up cleanly. Don't re-use birds and rabbits over and over again – in the field any dead game is picked up once and once only, and that's what we are practising. Bear in mind too, that many spaniels won't go back to dummy work again once they have picked the real thing, whether cold game or recently shot. So don't be in any rush to introduce your cold game, because you may find there is no going back! I sometimes want to demonstrate FTCh Abbeygale May (Tippy) to friends who are interested in her offspring, but this becomes a nightmare, as my so-called retired champion sits there sneering at the dummy I have thrown. One of her granddaughters was so uninterested in canvas that we had to soak a dummy in tripe juice – imagine what that was like at the end of a warm afternoon's training! So for me, the use of cold game should be fairly limited – as soon as your youngster has discovered how to pick it, you will be ready to go out shooting anyway.

Now that you have all aspects of the dog's future work in place, you can mock up the whole thing in the rabbit pen. Hide a dummy or cold rabbit in the corner of the pen as before. Get your youngster hunting and let him bolt a live rabbit. 'Shoot' the rabbit, and as long as the spaniel has been steady, send him back for the dummy or cold rabbit. When he brings it back you can congratulate yourself on reaching a major milestone – bar you actually shooting the rabbit, the spaniel has done everything that would be required out rough shooting. By the way, do avoid really shooting the rabbit pen bunnies; one novice found this a very expensive way of training his dog (and not entirely ethical!).

TROUBLE SHOOTING

My youngster seems very timid about actually flushing game

Don't worry too much about this, FTCh Gournaycourt Morag (Fudge) actually turned and ran the first time she flushed a pheasant but she still went on to come third in the Championships. Dogging-in on poults can be helpful, but it could also be that your dog is still just a little too young. If he really needs jazzing-up, throw an easy retrieve to the spot where the pheasant has just flushed and let the dog run in and pick it. Be careful not to 'punish' a dog unintentionally for flushing or bolting game. Often we are so keen to make sure the dog is steady that we come thundering down on it the second it has flushed the game. This gives the wrong message, so back off a bit – even if it means letting a youngster take a few steps towards the game, just blow the stop whistle calmly.

I can't get my dog to enter thicker cover

Keep a young dog away from really nasty cover like brambles or nettles, especially if there is no game in it. Many spaniels don't enter cover if there is no game scent. This is fine on a normal shooting day, but a real drawback if you want to compete. Even when you are not letting the youngster near live game, always hunt in cover that has game scent, and choose good scenting days for your hunting training. Use the dummy trick to encourage a youngster to get into cover. My very young pups go out on exercise with the trials dogs, so they get into the habit of following them into everything right from the beginning. Never, ever force a dog into cover.

My dog is good one day and bad the next

Or perhaps it is actually you being inconsistent with your training. Try to make all your training programme a smooth progression from one stage to the next. Don't be throwing in lots of different exercises into the mix, or moving on to a new lesson before the previous one has been fully learnt. When I started training Ricky, I was a bit over-keen and was teaching him a couple of different types of exercise alongside each other. Now I am plodding a bit more with him and he is much more settled.

My dog is fine with dummies, but he won't bring cold game back to me

A lot of youngsters do this at first, because the new prize is far too precious to bring straight back to the boss. A lot of Cocker bitches make off to the nearest ditch to bury it! This is one occasion where it is helpful to run away from the dog while blowing your return whistle. He should instinctively come to you, and because he wants it so much, he will bring the game with him. Don't be fooled into thinking he wants to give it to you though, and watch him closely with his game retrieving. When he does get up to you, don't be so anxious that you dash out and grab the game. Make the dog come and sit properly in front of you and deliver it correctly.

Part Two: Training and Working your Young Dog in the Field

9.
ROUGH SHOOTING WITH
NO ROUGH EDGES

Now that your dog has passed through basic training, there are four ways in which you can expect to be working him in the field. You can go rough shooting with him (and perhaps try field trialling). You can become a picker-up for driven shoots. You can beat on driven and semi-driven shoots. Or you can have him as your peg dog while you shoot on driven days. Nowadays, though, I think most of us would hope that our dog will actually become enough of an all-rounder to perform reasonably well in all these different disciplines of gundog work. Few of us have the luxury of a kennel full of specialist dogs, including everything from our Gordon Setter for grouse days to a magnificent black Lab of ancient bloodlines for a big driven pheasant shoot! Luckily for us, the spaniel (especially the Springer) has always been considered the most versatile of the gundog breeds.

The best way to start training your future all-round spaniel in the field is by taking him out on small, well-organised rough shooting-style training days, particularly on rabbits. When you first start working your spaniel on live game, and shooting that game for him to retrieve, is the big step change in your training programme. Up until now, most of your training has been a fairly private affair between you and the dog, most of it done in and around your home environment. If necessary, you can actually get this far without even using a rabbit pen – if you are inventive with tennis balls, the local wildlife and perhaps a bit of dogging-in. But now you and your dog are graduating from lessons 'in the classroom', to real working situations out there in the shooting field. For me, this is the big divide in gundog training. It isn't just the difference between 'theory' and 'practical'; it also tends to show up the gap between a novice trainer and the experienced or professional gundog handler.

Rough shooting over spaniels (CHARLES SAINSBURY-PLAICE)

Beginners are usually very successful with their dogs in early training. It is quite straightforward to get a book or some advice and gradually progress through all the various stages leading up to the real thing. I recently visited the 'Cockers-on-line' chat room (See Appendix III) where a lot of working Cocker first-timers discuss training issues. Many have backgrounds in other dog-world disciplines like obedience, agility and even showing. They are all bowled over by how quick their working Cockers are to learn the basics, and full of confidence about having a go at a bit of field trialling. But here comes the rub. Many have never actually been shooting, and have no idea of the transformation that can overtake a nicely obedience-trained dog once it gets into a hot shooting situation. All novice dog handlers – even those who are experienced shots and country dwellers – should be aware that paw perfect in the rabbit pen does not necessarily translate seamlessly into steady-as-a-rock on a contact flush with a cock pheasant. Nor does the ability to do a double back-flip with an assortment of dummies mean that the spaniel can do the same when presented with a wet hen pheasant runner hiding in a ditch.

Hence the need for a longish probationary period of continuing to train the youngster in controlled, but real shooting situations. And this is the other big divide between new handlers and established trainers – how can the beginner get access to this sort of shooting? When I was starting with spaniels back in the 1990s, all the books I read talked glibly of 'going out rabbiting with the young dog'. At the time, I was living in Kent on the edge of the North Downs, so there were certainly plenty of bunnies to be seen, hopping happily about on the close-cropped downland turf. The only trouble was that as soon as the dog and I set foot on a field, all the rabbits instantly disappeared into their many holes. The kind of rabbit you need for dog training is not a hole dweller, but instead uses 'seats' in small patches of rushes, gorse, brambles and even long grass. By and large this kind of rabbit has more or less disappeared over the last twenty years. You can find them in marshy or upland areas, mainly in Scotland, the north of England, the Welsh borders and a couple of secret places in the

Rough shooting over your own stylish spaniel makes all the training worthwhile
(NICK RIDLEY)

131

east Kent marshes. Even for professional trainers, access to these ideal rabbits is closely guarded, and the cause (almost literally!) of many a turf war.

The trouble with the training books of the last century is that they assume a wide availability of many forms of rough shooting, not just rabbiting, but walked-up pheasant shooting over dogs; upland hare and grouse shooting; even pigeon-flighting and wetland wildfowling. Since the huge boom in commercial driven shooting of the late 1980s and 1990s, coupled with intensive farming, these varieties of shooting are much in decline. It's hard even to bash a hedgerow these days when farmers are ploughing right into every corner of their fields, leaving nowhere for a bunny or a bird to hunker down. Incomprehensibly, this situation has actually been made worse by the constantly changing government regulations for set-aside and country stewardship. When my neighbour entered the stewardship scheme, I was delighted, imagining acres of conservation-friendly roughlands where I could work the dogs. Instead the farmer was given a grant to rip out several acres of upland gorse, bramble and rush, and to renovate some walling. Regardless of the loss of rough-shooting opportunities, almost every piece of government-sponsored farm management I have seen to date has been detrimental to wildlife conservation.

So, unless you are lucky enough to own land in the heart of the Pennines, or the Scottish Highlands, you won't be able to go it alone with your training any more. It's not a good idea at this stage anyway, because ideally you want to be part of a team of three or four people when you are out shooting for your dogs. At the very least you are going to need someone who knows a bit about rabbiting to shoot for you and your dog. I was very lucky when I started. Eric Burchell, a professional dog trainer, gave me some lessons and packed me off to Scotland to go field trialling. That was where I fell in with the Cocker gang – a really great bunch of people who were generous with both their time and their facilities (though I have yet to be initiated into some of those secret rabbit grounds!). Spaniel people being what they are, I'm sure you are already building your own network of dog training friends. Now you all need to get together to find some ground. With commercial driven shooting having gone into a slight decline, it is now much easier to buy small days for rough shooting training on a mixed range of quarry. Ask local keepers about the prospect of boundary days. Get everyone to club together to buy a fifty bird day. This works especially well if you have shooting but non-dog training friends who would appreciate a cheap day's shooting – the idea is that you work the dogs and they shoot.

Do be careful though about getting people involved who don't understand anything about dog training. If you are in a small syndicate for example, it's no good trying to convert them all to rough shooting overnight, so that you can train. Later on, when the dog is in great shape, you can suggest converting one of the less successful drives into walked-up, and then you can amaze them all with how great rough shooting is and how well your dog works.

First though, you need to practise. Assuming you and your training friends have found some suitable ground for training, hopefully it will have a few rabbits on it. In the early days of field training, rabbits are a much more suitable quarry than pheasants. Rabbits stay sitting in their seats, which means the dog has to work the scent thoroughly to find them. This encourages the youngster to develop a good, tight pattern. But pheasants usually run on, leaving a ground scent like a trail which the dog can just follow in a straight line. Too much work on pheasants which run like this can get the dog into the habit of pulling forward onto the scent, causing his pattern to deteriorate from a nice zig-zag into little more than a wiggly straight line. Another advantage of rabbits is that you can usually spot their seats yourself. If you see one, walk your dog away downwind, then turn and hunt into the wind towards the seat. This gives you a very controlled situation, which you are always looking for in training. Because you know where the rabbit is, you can be ready to take action in case the dog tries to run in. In the early days of your dog's training, you should always blow your stop whistle as he flushes game; he will pick up the habit of dropping to the flush quickly. If he manages to get away with running in or chasing it is hard to correct, but if it never gets into his head, he'll stay honest.

If he does run in, you must be ready to run after him and stop him at once. This is why to begin with you need to work the dog on a 'training shoot' rather than a normal shooting day. Obviously, you are stopping everything while you dash up to your dog to deliver a drubbing. This isn't going to go down very well on an ordinary shooting day! During training there are going to be moments when your young spaniel goes wrong. If this happens and you need to be in a situation where you can easily run after him and chastise him. When you reach him, grab him by the scruff or the jowl and drag him back to where he was when you blew the whistle. At the same time tell him off verbally and blow the stop whistle. He's been in the rabbit pen or similar often enough by now to know that he shouldn't be chasing. If he tries to chase again, don't let him hunt any more for the rest of the training session. Occasionally walk with your dog at heel just behind your training mate while he works his own dog. When your friend gets a flush, it will be less tempting for your dog, and also give you plenty of opportunity to ensure he is rock steady. But don't take the youngster out training again until you have done some more steadiness work at home.

133

If your young spaniel is being steady, and the resulting rabbits are successfully shot by you or a mate, don't get so excited that you end up letting the dog have loads of retrieves. Working on live game you still stick to the same principles as your dummy training. If you let your young spaniel have lots of easy retrieves of dead rabbits or marked birds lying out in the open it will go to his head. A good way to get round this is to work in partnership with your training mate. You can shoot over each other's dogs, which makes training a lot easier. When a rabbit is shot, you send your dog across for a bird his dog had originally bolted, and then he returns the favour. This not only gives the dogs a greater challenge in their retrieving, but also teaches them to be steady and patient while other dogs are working.

In the excitement of these first shooting days, it is easy to let aspects of the dog's work deteriorate, especially the hunting. With retrieving, you have organised it so that everything is very controlled and there is plenty of time for everyone to calm down, but when hunting, things can feel as though they are happening very quickly. A mistake some novices make, particularly if they have an athletic hunting dog, is to worry that everything will fall apart. They keep stopping and starting the dog because they are anxious about losing control. You have to try and be brave about this and let your flying machine do his stuff, even though it can feel like you are walking a tightrope. You are looking for a continuous, fluid action, with the dog flowing through and over the cover almost without pause. But don't make the mistake of walking faster and faster to try and keep up with the dog. That's when you get game flushing behind you, which is irritating for everyone. If your dog is pulling, cast him off into the wind, and as you walk, quietly drop some cold game or a tennis ball at your feet. Take a step or two backwards away from the ball and use your whistle to pip the dog back towards you. As he hunts into your feet he will get the reward of a find. After a few times he will realise that it's worth staying close to you.

Although pulling is a fault, it is often a sign that your young dog has a good nose. He's smelling game at a distance and is naturally keen to get on to it, rather than working his way there. Smell is a dog's dominant sense, so he will always go where his nose takes him. So don't forget everything we discussed in Chapter Four: *How to Hunt*. Now you are in a real hunting situation, it is more important than ever to be aware of scent, the wind and the impact they will have on your dog's hunting behaviour. Always try to hunt your young dog into

OPPOSITE: *Because the dog is steady to bolt a rabbit, it is safe to shoot ground game* (CHARLES SAINSBURY-PLAICE)

the wind. You need to keep checking whether the wind is coming from behind (a back wind) or the side (a cheek wind) or from directly in front. For an inexperienced dog the wind coming directly to him is the easiest to work and results in a classic quartering pattern with the dog zig-zagging in front of you. You want him to work a nice flat pattern quite close to you. That way he won't miss any game and you can keep eye contact and good control.

Now he's on open ground, instead of the confines of the rabbit pen, or cover you have carefully selected, the youngster may find it harder to keep an idea of exactly where the boundaries of his beat are, and where he should be going. You can give him some help with this by using your own body language. Begin by walking a bit of a zig-zag yourself and then gradually start going in a straight line as the dog gets the message. Dip your shoulder to the right or left, which gives him a good visual signal. You can use your hands, but you won't be able to do that if you are carrying a gun.

The other big new step forward your dog will have to take in his work now he is training in a live situation is with his retrieving. Up until now all his retrieves, even the long, blind and difficult ones, have been laid by you, exactly as you wanted them for training purposes. But in a real shooting situation, obviously the retrieves are going to be unpredictable. You can organise the easy ones as described above. What you now need to concentrate on is the type of retrieve that your dog will encounter a great deal in his career – birds whose fall he has marked but are not easy to find, or rabbits who have run on. If you have concentrated on your early retrieving exercises with dummies, you will be able to send your dog out in a straight line directly to the fall of the bird. Even if the bird (or rabbit) has run on wounded, your dog will be able to follow the line of the blood scent on the ground. So these marked but tricky retrieves shouldn't be a problem as long as you haven't skimped on the basic exercises, and can therefore send your dog out properly in the first place. As always, if things are going wrong, take a step back and work again on the early stages.

The most difficult retrieve is the truly blind, where the dog hasn't had a chance to mark the bird down and it has fallen in a difficult place. Often the spaniel didn't flush the bird in the first place, either because you have engineered it that way, or later on bigger shooting days this will happen anyway. This means your dog may not even be aware there is a bird to retrieve. The exercise of retrieving your friend's bird is useful to practise this, as are those early blind dummy retrieves. They will have given your dog the confidence to know that when you send him out for a retrieve, there will definitely be something to find. But your dog is going to need guidance from you in your handling. Good handling starts right from the beginning in how you send the dog out. You will know the general area where the bird fell, so you can point him in the right direction to begin with. Get him sitting attentively in front of you and then, with your hand and body language moving in the direction you want him to go, give him the verbal command.

It is important that your dog trusts you in this situation, so that he believes in the handling instructions you are giving him. You need to preserve this confidence by not crumbling yourself. In the stress of a difficult retrieve – especially if everybody is watching – you will be surprised how often even quite experienced handlers can go into panic mode. The whistle starts blowing, a stream of different commands comes thick and fast, and the hands wave like someone guiding in a jumbo jet to land. Most of the time the dog isn't even looking at the handler. If you want your dog to go where you point, it is

Keep in line with the Guns when rough shooting (CHARLES SAINSBURY-PLAICE)

137

fundamental that he is looking at you to see where you are pointing. So first of all, calm down. Blow the stop whistle so that the dog sits and looks at you – remember, if he doesn't stop on the whistle you must go back to your obedience work. Once he is sitting looking at you, take your time and decide exactly what it is you want him to do. Do you want him to come back to you so that you can start the retrieve from scratch? If so, blow the return whistle. Do you want him to get further back? Slowly and clearly give him your get out further command and, if it helps, a throwing out gesture with your hand. Does he need to come nearer and then take a different route? Blow the return whistle and let him come to where you want, then stop him again before giving him your right or left command.

If you are going to handle your dog well in these situations, there is one absolutely crucial piece of common sense that is forgotten about every day on the shooting field. You, the handler, need to know at least approximately where the bird is. On rough shooting days, when only one or two birds are being shot at a time, correct marking is much easier than when picking-up on a driven day (which we will discuss in the next chapter). So there is no reason for you not to have seen the bird fall or the rabbit shot. As you see that difficult bird fall, make a really good mark of where it lands. It's hard to believe when you are just reading about it, but under trying circumstances, it's all too easy to lose your mark. All the best dog handlers I have watched seem to have an internal sat-nav telling them exactly where to start the dog searching for the bird. The quicker you get the dog into the correct area, the easier it will be for him to find it. But be flexible too. With his superior scenting ability, even an inexperienced dog is more likely to know where the bird is than you are. So if he keeps pulling determinedly into a particular area, at least let him search it thoroughly before moving him elsewhere.

On hot days you and your training friends can vary your sessions by introducing water work. Find a lake or large pond with easy sloping sides and no dangerous areas. Reservoirs often have pumps which can create strong currents, while flooded quarries are dangerous for everyone because of their steep sides and cold, deep water. Make sure too, that your chosen lake isn't full of anglers or endangered wildfowl! Wear waders (or shorts if it's hot) so that you can walk into the water with a timid dog. Almost all spaniels enter water readily, but you will notice the more intelligent ones check carefully to make sure they have an exit route before they jump in. For straightforward retrieves, make sure you call the dog back just before he gets out of the water. Most dogs stop to shake when they reach the shore, and if you aren't calling them, they often put the dummy down before doing so – imagine if that was a wounded duck, you'd be right back at square one again! To help with steadiness, take a mixed group of young and trained dogs to the lake. Sit them all down on the edge. Then throw a dummy in the water and do some retrieving training with the older dogs. All the splashing and retrieving excites the youngsters, but they have to learn to sit and stay calm. It's also a great way of encouraging them to be quick into the water when their turn eventually does come.

Most top spaniel trainers continue to take their dogs on training days together right through their careers. I'm sure you will get into this habit as well; it's a really enjoyable way to work and train your dog. But the day will come when you are working your dog for other people to shoot over who are not dog-wise, possibly on a rough shoot you don't know. Things probably won't go as you plan. Stay calm. Work your dog extra close to you so that you have a greater chance of damage limitation (and of preventing either of you being shot!). Don't get bossy with the Guns when they start charging around, but don't be bullied by them either. If your dog needs a rest, give him one, no matter how much the excited Guns want to go on. And if a piece of ground looks too thick or dangerous, don't work it.

Most Guns brought up on driven birds are fairly inexperienced at rough shooting and don't realise that it needs a little discipline and common sense for it to be productive, enjoyable and safe. When you are shooting with inexperienced Guns, make sure there is someone in charge. Because rough shooting is informal we forget that it still needs a captain of the day. Decide before you start who it will be and then support him absolutely. That way everyone knows what they are doing and the opportunity for confusion or dispute is minimised. When you are working the dogs for other people, as opposed to on your own training day, you will have several Guns. Make sure they keep a straight line at right angles to the direction you are all walking. You must keep the line, even in woodland or when there is a hedge between you. Check each side of you, and if someone is getting too far ahead or behind, halt the line. A perfect line makes for great shooting because you can safely shoot behind as well as in front. Don't let people swing through the line. If someone is going to take a shot behind, they should take the gun out of their shoulder and not re-mount it until in a stable shooting position facing where they want to shoot.

On a rough-shooting day communication is even more important than with driven birds. As dog handler you should always tell the rest of the line what you are planning to do. If you are working one dog and you want to stop to change over and work another dog, explain it to everyone. There are terrible horror

Watch your dog's body language – a low position and plenty of tail action indicates game is close (NICK RIDLEY)

stories of handlers actually getting shot while changing dogs. If you are a Gun yourself, obviously you will be aware of dogs at work. Some handlers prefer you not to shoot too close to a young dog. It is also not considered good form to blaze away at birds or ground game flushed while a dog is working on a retrieve. Just make sure you know where the dogs are and what is happening. If you are with novice Guns, explain all this to them before you all set out. There's no need for anyone to be bossy about the basic safety rules. It's really just a matter of you all showing consideration for each other. And do stay calm. With dogs working and game everywhere, you'd be surprised how the adrenalin starts to pump. Staying cool improves your dog handling and your shooting.

A successful day's rough shooting over spaniels, with a mixed bag of perhaps wild pheasant, rabbit, pigeon and the odd partridge – all steadily flushed and efficiently retrieved – is among the best sporting fun you can have. And when it's your own spaniel, putting all his training into effect, it's magical. Some of my most memorable gundog moments have been on grouse in the Highlands, working my spaniels as a team with a couple of pointers. The spaniels walk to heel while the pointers make huge casts to find the grouse coveys. Once the pointer has gone on point we all rush over, ready to shoot. If the pointer is reluctant to flush, one my Cockers does the job. Then I can send another spaniel out for the retrieve. It is great fun, excellent training, and there's always grouse for supper!

TROUBLE SHOOTING

I can't find anywhere to train
You may have to be prepared to travel long distances to get the right ground for spaniel training. There are professional trainers based all over the country though, and booking yourself a few lessons is often the best way to cover this crucial period of training for the spaniel. You can usually track down a local trainer either through the sporting press or online.

My own shooting seems to go completely to pieces when I'm working the dog
This happens to most of us! While the dog is still in training, your full concentration will inevitably be on him, rather than on your shooting. Get a friend to do as much of the shooting as possible, and even when your dog is trained, be prepared for it to take a while for both you and the dog to achieve your peak performance!

I've started working my dog on a rough shoot but the general gundog work is awful, and the Guns shoot anything that moves
When you start out working your spaniel, it pays to be careful in the company you keep. Wild dogs will lead yours astray, and wild Guns are dangerous. Don't be so desperate to work your dog that you will take him anywhere – you will soon stop enjoying your sport.

Now that I've started shooting with my youngster I'm finding him very hard to control
Working good, keen young spaniels can be like walking a tightrope. Concentrate on what you are doing and give the dog firm leadership. If he shows signs of unsteadiness, drop back and do a lot more steadiness training. But as long as he isn't being unsteady, keep your nerve and don't try to slow him down too much.

Always watch your dog carefully when he is on a retrieve
(CHARLES SAINSBURY-PLAICE)

10.
PICKING-UP WITHOUT TEARS

With today's rather limited opportunities for rough shooting, picking-up on a driven shoot is likely to be one of your main opportunities for starting off your young spaniel in the field. This area of work is probably the biggest source of 'job opportunities' for gundogs these days, whether Labrador or spaniel. So once you have completed your spaniel's basic education, got him steady, and given him his experience in the rabbit pen, dogging-in and out on a few rough shooting training days, it is very likely that a day picking-up on the local driven shoot (often a commercial one) will be the dog's next experience in the field. Congratulations on getting your youngster to this stage successfully, but without wishing to sound too negative, prepare yourself for a big disappointment. Picking-up ain't what it used to be.

The pressure of commercial driven shooting is pushing the art of picking-up farther and farther back against the wall. On large shoots which need to be profitable, overstretched keepers want as many birds as possible picked as quickly as possible. The luxury of leaving the picking-up of all but the runners to the end of the drive has all but disappeared. Instead pickers-up are encouraged to stand far back from the line and work their dogs throughout the drive, with all the chaos that ensues. Because the pickers-up are working during the drive they can't stay with their dogs, as that would mean moving around among the Guns. So the dogs are inevitably working at a further distance than their handlers can really manage, and with all the noise of the shooting and distractions of birds falling, whistle, voice and hand commands are ineffective. In practice therefore, picking-up on many shoots basically means letting the dogs off and hoping they keep re-appearing with another retrieve. I'm afraid on the average driven shoot you can come across an enormous number of faults in the dog work. There will be dogs switching from one retrieve to another, or 'blinking' (running past without retrieving) some birds, and there will certainly be dogs running in. This last is particularly frustrating for Guns with peg dogs. As you will discover, it takes two or three years to train a steady peg dog, but only one shooting day when other dogs nick his retrieves from under his nose, to ruin him.

Obviously you can't let your good young spaniel get involved in this mayhem, or you will undo all your last eighteen months of training. When you are a Gun, the solution is simple. You just leave the dog in the vehicle during drives and wait for a more suitable day to work your dog. But if you are meant to be picking-up (and perhaps getting paid for it), the situation is a lot trickier. Certainly you can't let your part-trained dog join in a free-for-all but nor do you want to be considered stand-offish or not earning your pay. This is partly where field trialling dogs acquire a reputation for being useless on a 'real shoot' – it's more that their handlers can distinguish between disciplined dog work and a mêlée, and are naturally wary of the latter.

So how can you do your share without ruining your dog? At the beginning the best solution is to ask the keeper to let you work at the back alongside the 'sweeper'. The sweeper role is pretty much the same as in soccer. It's usually taken by a highly experienced handler with more than one dog, who acts as the last line of defence, concentrating on runners and hit birds that have eventually fallen a long way back. Sweepers tend to operate as loners, often staying behind after everybody else has moved on to the next drive. This will keep your dog away from the worst rough and tumble, as well as giving you the opportunity to practise difficult retrieves – and almost certainly to learn from a master; sweepers are the A-list of pickers-up. During your first season of picking-up try to cultivate a reputation for good dog work and good communication in order to gain the respect of the keeper and captain of pickers-up. If they like what you are doing, they will be more receptive to your working how you want to work. But remember, it's not your job to change the world. If the canine chaos seems inescapable, just quietly put your own dog back on his slip. If you have a choice of shoots to pick up on, try to get yourself off the list of those where the work is poor. But on a high quality shoot make yourself indispensable to the keeper. Volunteer for the jobs no one else wants, arrive early and leave late. Gradually you will manoeuvre yourself into a position where you can work your dog at a good level and learn from some top handlers.

Picking-up is unlike other aspects of dog work because it requires a great deal of interaction with people, as well as with your dog. When you are training your dog, and even when rough shooting over him, it is really just the pair of you doing your own thing. But when you are a picker-up, all this changes. You are answerable to the captain of pickers-up and to the keeper, and also to the shoot owner or host and his guests, the Guns. It isn't very egalitarian I'm afraid, but the etiquette is important for a number of reasons. A driven shoot is not a training day (unless you and your friends have bought it for that very purpose). You are being employed to work your dog, not to train him or have a bit of fun with him. Very often the team of Guns and/or their host will be paying considerable amounts of money for the day. It costs a Gun between £30 and £40 to shoot a pheasant, and if that Gun has a dog and he wants his dog to retrieve that bird, he isn't going to take too kindly to you sending your dog to snatch £40 worth of pheasant from under his nose. So if you see that the Gun standing in front of you has a peg dog, make yourself known to him before the start of the drive, and ask what his plans are. A lot of Guns don't have any plans, but at least you've asked! Try to work with the Gun and communicate rather than being defensive or territorial – a trap a lot of pickers-up fall into. You should never assume all Guns are 'the enemy' – they may be picking up behind you another day.

While the drive is on, do count how many birds are down in your area, and which ones run on. In Europe the pickers-up have a notebook and even draw diagrams of where birds fall. Don't work your dog during the drive unless you are well back from the line and have been asked to concentrate on runners and distant fallers by the picking-up captain or the keeper. Once you start the retrieving, remember to keep a close watch on your dog at all times – the worst sin a picker-up can commit is to stand around chatting with mates while the dog is working. Don't let your dog drop retrieves, or switch from retrieve to retrieve, as this leads to birds being 'blinked' by other dogs. Be honest if your dog misbehaves in any way. If he happens to peg a bird (retrieve an unharmed bird) you must tell the keeper. It's no good hoping no one will notice, some Guns can be very eagle-eyed when there's money involved. Tell the picking-up captain or keeper if you think there is a bird unaccounted for by the time you are needed to move on to the next drive, then the sweeper or you can stay behind for it.

Another surprising source of non-retrieving problems when you first start picking-up with your youngster can come from his relations with other dogs on the shoot. If you only have one dog, the sheer number of dogs he will meet on a driven shoot can be quite a shock, even if you and he have been on training days with other dog handlers. One of the most difficult moments is when you all pile into the pickers-up truck together and a couple of the dogs take a dislike

Using the 'stop' hand signal on a retrieve ...

... and then following it with a directional hand signal (CHARLES SAINSBURY-PLAICE)

to each other. The problem of a dog that is aggressive with other dogs on the shoot can be difficult to cure. But look for underlying causes. Is the dog insecure? Are you giving firm leadership? You need to be the one in charge, if the dog respects you, then all the problems can be corrected. Unintentionally you could also be giving the wrong firm leadership! Dogs are very quick to pick up on human interactions, so if there is someone you don't like very much on the shoot, your dogs are likely to feel the same way about each other. At one shoot, one of the other lady Guns and I were very polite to each other, but we were always going to be chalk and cheese. Our dogs naturally felt the same way – but expressed it rather less politely, though of course we all pretended we didn't notice it!

Hopefully though, having negotiated the various pitfalls of picking-up etiquette, the main thing you will be concentrating on is the quality of your dog's retrieving work. Obviously you must make sure he has no faults. He must be steady, and not run in, just as you have taught him in training. He should retrieve the bird you tell him too, even when there are lots of dogs running around hoovering up birds randomly. He should bring it back to you swiftly without mouthing it or dropping it at any stage. Then he should sit and wait for you to send him before going for another retrieve. Particularly in the early days, never send him for lots of retrieves. Pick up the easy dead birds yourself after the drive, and just concentrate on the fewer, but more difficult retrieves.

These tricky retrieves make picking-up worth doing. The challenge of finding a strong runner, or putting your dog on exactly the right spot for a long blind retrieve, is great fun, and very rewarding when you get it right. Yet it is a part of dog work which many novice handlers find the most difficult of all. I probably get more queries to my gundog column in *The Field* about retrieving problems than I do even about steadiness. Perhaps it is because a failed retrieve is so obvious. Where steadiness is usually a matter of degree for amateurs who can live with 'steady enough', retrieving is very black and white – either you found and picked up the bird or you didn't. For most everyday gundog owners who are not interested in trialling their spaniels, retrieving is also likely to be the main thing their dog is called upon to do. For the rough shooter (or field trialler), the retrieve is the icing on the cake after the all-important process of hunting and flushing and being steady to the game. But the picker-up's dog isn't required to do any of those things; he's just needed for retrieving – and if he gets that wrong, then you really may as well go home.

With all the pressure they are putting themselves under, it's hardly surprising that novice pickers-up can get quite harassed about difficult retrieves, often making the most simple and basic errors that they would never do at home. So when you are faced with difficult retrieves, or runners which have been lost, the first thing to do is stay calm and keep your common sense switched on. On my own shoot last season I took a couple of my Cockers back to help another spaniel handler look for two very strong runners which had been seen to leg it into the wood during the drive. Nobody had any real mark on these birds, and it was in any case highly unlikely that they were still sitting where last seen. So I was very surprised to see the spaniel man constantly pipping and giving hand signals to his dog, who was quartering the ground close to him. The keeper explained that this chap was a great dog man who hunted his dog nice and close to him. Which would have been fine if we had been hunting, but we were retrieving! The handler's common sense had deserted him, and he was treating the ground as if it was a beat stuffed with live game for his dog to hunt up. Instead he should have been letting his dog range out long and wide with minimal interference from him. I told my Cocker 'get out' so he knew he was searching for a blind retrieve rather than hunting live game. He went out a good 100 metres and began making sweeps back towards me, scenting the wind as he turned. I didn't give him any signals or commands, because I had less idea where the bird might be than he did, but I watched him very closely. Soon enough I saw my dog's nose whip round and he made a dash out to the side. He'd found the scent trail and was lining it – definitely not the time to pip him back! So I let him do his thing and pretty soon he had rugby tackled a very strong cock pheasant and brought it back. It had been wing-shot and would have been perfectly capable of running and walking for miles. Not the kind of bird you are going to find by hunting your dog at your feet.

So take a moment before you start on a retrieve to think about what you are doing. Are you sweeping for a runner or runners? Nobody really knows where these birds are, so there's no point giving your dog a lot of commands. Just get him out there searching. Or is it a dead bird which you have actually been able to mark down into a particular area? In this situation you can help your dog by giving him very clear direction, working him in just the way you have practised on dummies all this time. Whenever you have to handle a dog out to a particular area, remember to be calm, slow and deliberate in your commands and signals.

You can make picking-up much easier for you and the dog by doing some basic preparations before the drive even starts. As you take up your position, make a little mental map to yourself of the area you are covering. Where are the birds likely to fall? If it is a high bird shoot or the wind is behind the birds, notice it, because it means the birds will fall further back than usual, even when dead. Are there any ditches, drains or bits of deep cover nearby that a wounded bird would be likely to run into? Remember, a winged bird still has the full use of its legs and can run unseen along a ditch for a long way. As the drive progresses, do keep an eye on apparently dead birds. Very often a bird seems to hit the ground like a stone but suddenly recovers half-way through the drive and legs it into the wood.

Most important of all, you must get a good mark on a fallen bird. Poor marking is one of the commonest causes of failed retrieves. I see this all the time on shoots. The handler sends the dog to a certain spot, but comes up with nothing. Handlers are always asking me why the dog failed on the retrieve. Yet again the answer is down to the most basic common sense. The dog didn't retrieve the bird, because – guess what – the bird wasn't there, and nine times out of ten, the bird wasn't there in the first place. If you tell your dog to go where the bird isn't, then surprise, surprise, there won't be a bird for him to retrieve, so you will have a 'failed' retrieve. Your dog relies on your handling and if you have told him to go to the wrong place, the most well-trained dog in the world won't come back with the bird. So good marking makes for good retrieving.

Learn to mark properly using fixed landmarks you can see from all around. Perfect your marking techniques. This will improve your retrieving as much as any amount of training. Use not one but two stationary landmarks to triangulate the fallen bird. For example: ten metres in front of the stump, on a line with the gate at the side of the field. Then if you move while looking for the bird, you will still have a good mark. Choose sensible landmarks. An experienced field trialler once confessed to me that he'd marked a bird as being beside a sheep – this in a field of perhaps two hundred sheep. Practise your marking while you are out strolling with your dog. Hide a tennis ball at the beginning of the walk, mark it carefully and continue with your ramble. On your way back see whether you can put the dog exactly on the ball.

One thing a picker-up learns early on is never to rely on other people's marks. Guns are notoriously over-enthusiastic and random in their marking, especially if they don't work a dog themselves. Usually a picker-up can safely assume that the bird a Gun tells her is lying dead over here, has in fact long since got up and run to over there. Guns assume everything they have shot at is dead and they never really know where it fell. Ian Openshaw once told me of picking-up: 'Believe half of what you see and nothing of what you hear. When it comes to marking fallen game that's the best advice there is.' In fairness to Guns they are often moving and turning on a bird far more than they realise. And once they

Use the left hand to stop the dog if you are going …

... to signal left (CHARLES SAINSBURY-PLAICE)

have fired, their attention rapidly goes back to the flushing point for the next bird, while behind them the 'stone dead' bird has risen with all the vigour of Lazarus and legged it to the nearest piece of cover.

So there will be times when you are trying to handle your dog into the area indicated by the Gun who marked the bird, and everything goes completely pear-shaped as the dog insists on dashing off elsewhere. Don't panic. Remember the most common cause of failed retrieves? Bird not there. Don't fall into the trap of sending the dog back again and again into that very same spot where the bird isn't and perhaps never was. It is likely that the bird has run, or even more likely that the bird was never where the Gun 'marked' it in the first place! Especially if your dog is keen to go and hunt a different area, trust his judgement – he may be getting the scent from where the bird has actually fallen as opposed to where the humans think it has fallen. Instead of sending your dog repeatedly into a particular area just on someone else's say so, work with your dog. Let him hunt widely and watch closely for any signs that he may have found the fall or a line – anything to give you a clue of where the bird may really be.

151

Be alert to what your dog is doing from the moment you send him out. Sometimes you can have a problem even getting the dog into the area you want. If you are having trouble getting your dog to work a certain area, it is worth asking yourself why this might be so, because it is usually a symptom of some other problem with the retrieve. This goes back to the issue of whether the bird is there in the first place. If it isn't and the dog has a good idea of where it is, naturally that is where the dog will go, regardless of all your whistling. Watch your dog carefully and get an understanding of his behaviour and body language. It is usually pretty obvious when a dog finds a fall or comes across a line. Trust him and let him work out that bit of scent before you handle him somewhere else.

Situations can change very rapidly when you are picking-up, so you have to keep thinking about what you are doing all the time. Sometimes you will send your dog to the fall of a dead bird that you both marked, and yet it seems to have disappeared into hyperspace – more likely the nearest ditch. Don't dismiss the idea that it may have run just because it looked dead when it fell. It keeps coming back to the basic point that if you are not finding a bird, it's usually because the bird isn't there, so you have to keep your mind open to alternative possibilities. Be ready to change your tactics when necessary.

Less often you will find yourself in the opposite situation, where you send your dog for a bird that is lying in the open for all to see, yet he just goes straight past it. This usually happens when the retrieve is 'scent blind' for some reason – it may be lying in a puddle or in a dip where the wind is going over the top of it. Scent can be spoiled by water, roads, paths, human traffic and animals, so an apparently easy retrieve may well be harder than it looks. Your dog always trusts his nose before his eyes. Even though he can see the bird, because he can't smell it, he doesn't believe it is the retrieve you want. You will have to encourage him verbally. I say something like: 'There, bring it in' and this usually works. It helps to teach your dog this in advance on dummies. Just incorporate it into your training from time to time and he will get the idea very quickly.

When picking-up – and in fact with all aspects of dog work – try to think dog. If you know that he has fallen short on a retrieve because his low eye line means it is hidden from him, then you will also know the answer: to him it is a blind rather than a seen retrieve. Now you can react accordingly. As you can commence a retrieve, ask yourself a few questions. Can the dog see it? Can the dog smell it? Was it really dead? Was it marked correctly? Have you found the fall? Is there a line? Where is the wind blowing? Is the dog working with you? Are you handling correctly? Almost every time, the answer to one of these questions will help you solve the retrieve.

A successful retrieve (CHARLES SAINSBURY-PLAICE)

TROUBLE SHOOTING

My dog mouths the bird and doesn't pick it up cleanly

Overcoming this is very simple if your dog is on the whistle properly. As soon as he starts to pick the bird up, blow your return whistle, and he won't have time to think of playing with the bird because he will be busy coming back to you with it. When you first start shooting with your dog you can help prevent the mouthing problem by avoiding difficult carries like big cock pheasants or well-grown rabbits and hares. Instead, work the dog on younger rabbits, partridges and hen pheasants so that he gets into the habit of an easy, swift pick up and a quick run back to you.

153

My dog retrieves fine, but puts the bird down when he is still a few feet from me
A good way of encouraging a dog's retrieving is to hide so that he needs to come running to try and find you. You can also get down low to make yourself more inviting. Don't go running up to him and pull the bird out of his mouth, this will just reinforce him into stopping early and dropping it.

My youngster doesn't seem very keen about picking-up
And very wise he is too! Don't let him run about with other picking-up dogs, and don't let him go for loads of easy seen retrieves. Instead work him very selectively on difficult blind or running birds which will challenge him and get him interested. With a hot dog you would stay away from runners, but with a sticky dog who isn't keen, a runner is a good way of firing his enthusiasm.

I'm having a lot of difficulty handling my dog on retrieves
Most likely a sign that you need to step back a stage. It may be too early for your youngster to take the added pressures of a real shooting situation. Go back to dummies and a little rough shooting or rabbit pen work until he is more mature.

11.
BEATING BUT NOT BEATEN

Experienced dog handlers say that the worst thing you can do with a promising youngster is take it beating. Unfortunately, not only is it the worst, but also the first thing many novice spaniel trainers do when their young dogs are ready to enter the field. There is often so little hunting work to be had for your spaniel that it's all too easy to fall into the trap of thinking that going beating could be the answer. Finding rabbiting, and the kind of small, walked-up days that are ideal for training the young spaniel in the field can be really difficult. Buying such days does also cost a bit, so the idea of beating – for which you will even get pocket money and certainly a free lunch – is very tempting. And there will be plenty of keepers dangling that temptation in front of you. Once it is known you have a decent dog, the offers of beating come in thick and fast. If you hope your dog will mature into a versatile, obedient animal that can do anything from sitting on the peg to bolting a rabbit, these offers should be resisted.

Beginners imagine that they will have a chance to hunt their youngsters nicely, working on their quartering, just as they have been doing in the rabbit pen. But you shouldn't get carried away with the idea that beating will give you an opportunity to practise the dog's hunting. Beating is very different from proper dog work. In fact I often wonder why modern driven shoots even bother with dogs in the beating line. In the past – and still in parts of Europe today – beating was performed by men, and often boys, using sticks, rattles and clappers. With wild birds on a sparsely populated shoot simulating more 'natural' conditions, dogs are essential, first to find the birds and then flush them effectively. But on modern driven shoots, especially the big commercial ones using only released poults, the birds are usually fairly tightly packed in one area, the chosen holding cover. If you walk a line of people abreast through that cover, nearly all the birds will be flushed without any need for dogs. Hard-hunting dogs in the line are actually a disadvantage in this situation. Depending on the wind and weather conditions there will be a great tendency for birds either to flush all at once (reducing the opportunity for Guns to shoot them) or to run ahead for ages and only flush late in the drive, making for poor shooting.

Yet we still seem to be very hung up on the idea that there should be loads of spaniels running around in front of a team of beaters. Really they shouldn't be there, and your properly trained young dog definitely shouldn't be there either. But human nature being what it is, we all want our dogs to come with us and take part in whatever we are doing. Especially if you plan for your spaniel to become an all-rounder, beating will eventually be one of his duties. But certainly don't rush into going beating. If you are already a regular beater, don't take your dog with you at all during his first shooting season.

The problem for the novice, training his young dog through his first season in the field, is that beating is purely functional. There is almost no training impact to be gained from it, and on the contrary, there is a very high risk of beating inducing faults in an inexperienced spaniel. Beating with a youngster will certainly make him harder to steady. There is also a danger that he will get the chance to peg game, that is, to catch a rabbit or pheasant before it has had an opportunity to bolt/flush. He may even be exposed to other dogs who are making a noise, and this particular fault spreads like wildfire among dogs. You will have been working hard for a year to produce a young dog with none of these faults – but after just one day beating you could easily find yourself with a dog showing signs of becoming a real sinner!

Because beating is a form of hunting up game, there is a widespread impression that the way spaniels run around when beating is the way they should be worked. As someone interested in good dog work, it is easy to see how far from the ideal beating is. When your dog is hunting correctly, his job is to produce the game for you to shoot easily and safely. So he has to quarter close to you, missing no game and flushing birds well within range, then dropping while you shoot. But when the dog is working in a beating line, all he is doing is driving game towards a waiting team of Guns who may not even be in sight. Few beating lines give him an opportunity to quarter properly. Game is usually bumped up by general disturbance rather than being genuinely flushed by the dog, and if he is lucky enough to get a contact flush, the line won't stop long enough for him to drop.

Worse still, the beating line will be populated by wild-eyed dogs completely

Take your thumbstick with you when beating (CHARLES SAINSBURY-PLAICE)

157

out of control, whose only aim is to get to the other end of the drive as quickly as possible. And sadly, it is very unlikely that you will find fellow gundog trainers among the beaters. Instead you are likely to meet quite a negative reaction to your efforts to keep your dog steady. You will hear remarks like, 'that dog's holding us back', or 'these field trial people are useless when it comes to real shooting'. For me, it just isn't worth the hassle, so I avoid beating. But I am lucky enough to have my own shoot, which makes it a lot easier to be superior about beating! A lot of us are on stand-and-walk shoots, where taking your turn in the beating line is unavoidable. And if you need to keep on good terms with the gamekeeper in order to preserve your dogging-in opportunities, there are going to be times when you have no choice but to beat.

However, there are ways you can make this situation slightly less desperate – and even put in a little secret steadiness training. Don't make a big deal of it with the other beaters though. If it isn't already well known that you are trying to train your dog properly, don't mention what you are doing. Have a thumb-stick or similar walking stick with you when you are beating. When the beating line starts moving, take your place in it (preferably at one end) and walk along with everyone – but keep your dog to heel. Use your stick to stir up any sticky birds. Keep your whistle in your mouth and your eyes on the dog, and be ready just in case he is unsteady. If you get challenged for keeping your dog at heel – which may well happen – then you can hunt him in a pattern that is very close and tight. Make sure you keep him very flat, that is, have your dog passing in front of you right at your feet. This will help prevent him getting too hot and pulling on or chasing. If the line is going too slowly for your strong hunting dog, then send him out wider side to side of you, rather than let him pull on in front. All the other dogs will be running on ahead in straight lines, missing tons of game and being generally wild.

Concentrate on keeping your youngster as steady as possible. Ignore stares you may get from the keeper and continue to hunt him really close to you. With any luck this will mean he doesn't get any flushes, as all the birds will have been put up long since by the rampaging beaters and dogs. If he does happen to nose out a bird and it flies, blow the stop whistle, then say firmly 'gone away'. This is the signal to the dog that there will be no retrieve arising from that particular flush. Make sure the dog drops for an instant before whistling him back to you. If he doesn't drop, don't worry, just pip him straight back to your feet and have him to heel for a few strides so that you re-establish control.

You will almost certainly come across a bird that runs on in front of the dog, rather than flushing. Obviously don't let your dog chase it. Equally, don't let

When he has a flush out beating, keep walking and pip your dog back to you
(NICK RIDLEY)

him take its line. This is when the dog stops quartering and instead follows just the straight line of scent left behind by the running bird. Tell your dog 'leave that' and pip him back to you before casting him out again in the opposite direction from where the bird ran. If you come across sticky birds, try to use your thumbstick to flush them if you can – you don't want your youngster to get a chance to peg. If the nightmare happens and your dog chases, there is nothing you can do. Certainly don't run after him, and don't keep pipping the whistle. When he re-appears, put him back on the slip-lead. You will have to take him back into the rabbit pen in the morning to re-establish his steadiness. From now on, you really need to try to avoid beating!

A dog that has spent too much time beating will usually become too head-strong to shoot over successfully. It is especially important to be fully aware of these danger areas if you are bringing up your youngster to be an all-rounder. Beating, heavy drives, too much retrieving and too much game are the things most likely to send your versatile youngster off the rails. It's quite likely that at this stage in your training programme, you will suddenly become much more aware of all the different kinds and grades of game shooting going on in the UK. Guns without dogs tend to be much less discerning about shoots and how they are managed than people who are handling a dog. I noticed this myself. Having spent several years shooting on expensive, large bag, high driven bird shoots, I tended to judge my day's sport by how well the birds had flown, how well I had shot, and possibly by the size of the bag.

Once I started working a dog as well as shooting, I suddenly became aware of a great range of other factors in the day's shooting. Picking-up after the drive, I noticed for the first time that many birds are in fact pegged rather than being shot, especially when the pickers-up sweep through a release pen where weaker birds will still be sitting. I saw that an equal number of birds are not retrieved – either because they have run or been mis-marked, or because dogs have picked and then dropped them. As I got more experienced and concentrated more on my dog work, I gradually became aware of the general level of incompetence – not to say outright chaos – that is sometimes going on around a team of paying Guns who are completely oblivious to it! I think the main reason for this dates back to the boom in commercial, driven, large-bag days during the 1980s and 1990s, which changed the whole picture of dog work. Guns then were often inexperienced, and in their quest for more and higher birds, the percentage of wounded runners to retrieve on each drive increased. Combined with this, the new breed of urban-dwelling Gun tended not to have dogs or to know much about what went on behind the scenes during a shoot. The commercial shoots were under tremendous pressure both to show and bag very large numbers of birds. At the same time they were able to get away with dodgy dog work which more experienced Guns would not have tolerated.

In the beating line spaniels bred and trained to flush perhaps ten birds over the course of one drive were being allowed to run riot through cover into which hundreds of immature slow-flushing birds had been released. Unsurprisingly, chasing, speaking and even pegging became rife. So today we are in a situation where a whole new generation of Guns, shoot owners and even gamekeepers has grown up with very little experience of what good dog work is like, or any understanding of why we should recognise and discourage faults. As you continue to train and work your good spaniel in the field, this culture of sloppy dog work is likely to become irritating. At a personal level you need to be tolerant, but as far as the dog is concerned, the problem is that gundog faults are very contagious. It is extremely difficult to train a dog to work well as an all-rounder on a shoot where the general level of dog work is poor.

Running-in is one of the most common faults you will see on driven shoots, as well as being one of the fundamentals. It isn't a matter of being some kind of 'field trial snob' – running-in poses a big danger to the dog, which may well be mistakenly shot at or injured in some other way while it is running around uncontrolled. This is why so many shoots deny Guns the old-fashioned pleasure of the safe shot that puts a rabbit or hare in the bag. With a lot of unruly dogs

With an inexperienced dog get the keeper to let you work on the edge of the line so he doesn't see too much of the action (NICK RIDLEY)

darting about it is just too risky. Since dogs are pack animals, speaking is extremely infectious. A background of constant yapping is annoying not just for the Guns but everyone involved in the day. More importantly though, even the doziest of game will eventually get the message and push off elsewhere. So there are very good reasons why faults should not be allowed in dog work. For example, a hard-mouthed retrieve results in an inedible bird. Dogs being out of control in the beating line increases the likelihood of birds leaking out to the side of the drive or flying backwards, which means fewer birds being put over the Guns. A big flush of birds is usually caused by dogs chasing in the beating line, and again decreases the percentage of birds actually shootable for the Guns.

Controversy over this situation is growing in the sporting press. Many of the country's leading younger shots are moving back towards walked-up shooting and small, wild bird shoots. Changes in government regulations over medicating and releasing poults are also having an impact. So the situation may well improve. But for the time being, the novice handler trying to train his young dog in the field just has to make the best of things. Whatever your opinion of the dog work on a particular shoot, don't voice it – unless it is good! Instead find small shoots where there is respectable dog work. It helps if the keeper is a keen dog handler or field trialler, although these are in the minority. When you find yourself on a shoot with dodgy dogs, just try to protect your youngster as far as possible, and avoid that shoot in the future. As long as you are tactful with your fellow dog handlers, and careful with your dog's steadiness, it is possible to make the best of things when going beating.

TROUBLE SHOOTING

There are very few spaniels on my shoot, so the keeper is always wanting me to work mine non-stop

This is a common problem for a man with a good dog! Springers especially are at a premium, particularly on shoots with a lot of thick, rough cover. Volunteer to sweep up runners at the end of the drive, as this will mean you won't have finished in time to beat during the next drive. It has been known for hard-pressed spaniel trainers to invent the occasional runner to take them away from the thick of the action.

One of the beaters' dogs barks whenever it flushes a bird

Try to keep yourself on the opposite end of the line from the noisy dog. Avoid your own dog having any contact flushes while you are beating. If you see a bird, flush it yourself with your stick. But in the long term, this may be a shoot you have to abandon if you are serious about having a top class, steady, all-round spaniel.

Our beating line goes so fast I'm always noticing us walking over birds
Actually, from a training point of view, this isn't the end of the world. Just keep your dog to heel and walk at the same pace as the rest of the line. If your dog isn't hunting, at least he isn't being spoiled!

The keeper's spaniel chases almost every drive, should I say something?
Definitely not. As long as birds are going into the bag, many gamekeepers are not at all interested in what the dogs are doing. But do see if you can find a shoot with a better attitude to dog work.

12.
PAW PERFECT ON THE PEG

If you are ever short of a topic to get the conversation going among a group of gundog trainers, just pose this question: 'Which is more likely to ruin a young dog: beating or sitting on the peg?' Keen field triallers wouldn't do either with their spaniel until after it has retired from competition. But for most shooting folk, their dog is a companion who is also useful. He's there to cheer us up on bad days and applaud us on good days, and if he can hunt and flush and retrieve birds to a reasonable standard, so much the better. Naturally we are going to want him with us sitting on the peg when we go driven shooting. Unfortunately, from a training point of view there's nothing natural about it, especially when it comes to spaniels.

For 95 per cent of spaniels, sitting on a peg doing nothing is the hardest task of all. So, if you are planning that your spaniel should be purely a peg dog, be aware that you are going against the grain. There is a fashion among aristocrats to have Cockers as their peg dogs, but really, unless you have your own grouse moor, it's a bit of an affectation. Ian Openshaw explains: 'With a peg dog a lot of the time your dog is there just as an accessory. You want your dog as a companion that is not going to get in the way or make a noise when you are on a hot peg or enjoying a drink with your fellow guns. Genuine, bomb-proof gentlemen's peg dogs like this are hard to find.'

So don't expect your dog to be able to perform this role perfectly at eighteen months old in his first season shooting. It will take about four years before a dog can become that mature and reliable. The good news is that there is no secret to the training. It is just patience and consistency followed by more

---

OPPOSITE: *The dog should sit at your feet watching you* (CHARLES SAINSBURY-PLAICE)

patience and consistency. The bad news is that doing it properly is very boring. You simply teach the dog to sit stay and walk at heel on command no matter what else is going on around it. If it moves a muscle on the sit you must step in and reprimand it. This means that you are going to need eyes in the back of your head when shooting for the next couple of years.

When we first choose a pup or a young dog to train on, the things we all get excited about are drive and style, but that's exactly what you don't want in a peg dog. Youngsters that grow up to be good peg dogs are really the kind of dogs that you wouldn't pick to train because they are so boring. They don't have loads of brains and initiative, nor do they look amazing. Instead the ideal peg dog should be naturally laid-back and patient. He will need to be an easy-going placid dog, a fire-and-forget model. This kind of dog also makes an ideal family dog. If your spaniel is going to be in the house with you, and possibly even have a role as a family pet as well as a shooting dog, then this is one area where input from the family will help rather than hinder.

A good peg dog has the capacity to switch off, no matter what his surroundings. So if he can relax and sit quietly while the family is bombing around the house and the Wii games console is in full flow, it is likely that he will be able to do the same while sitting on a peg. Of course, very few spaniels do have that kind of temperament. Howard Day describes having a Cocker in the house as, 'like the wall of death, this dog is zooming round the room at apparently head height – and they never stop.' But if you do have the kind of spaniel that isn't interested in hunting, or could even be described as lazy, peg work could very well turn out to be his niche. Recruit the family to take him all over the place, and if you have the kind of job that allows, take him with you to work.

Learning to sit still and do nothing in all circumstances for long periods of time is the fundamental for a dog who is going to be first and last a peg dog. Ian Openshaw agrees: 'If you want to end up with a really steady peg dog, you must be prepared to bore it and maybe yourself to death, which is a shame if your dog turns out to be a flyer with a lot of drive and intelligence.' That's where the rub comes in. Hopefully by this stage in your dog's training, you will have discovered that a good spaniel does far more than just sit there! It's when you own a dog with genuine ability that you start wanting to do a lot more with him. But working a dog as an all-rounder is asking him big questions. A dog that has the drive to hunt cover; the intelligence to work with scent; the obedience to be handled on a retrieve; and the patience to sit quietly on a peg is very rare – and such talented dogs usually end up being field trialled.

So training your young dog for the peg as well all his other work is going to be a challenge for both of you. But the reward – owning a competent, reliable all-rounder spaniel – is well worth it. When my spaniels retire from field trialling they cease to be specialist dogs and come with me everywhere I go shooting, whether it's walking up grouse in the Highlands or a big driven pheasant day in Devon. Last season I had FTCh Abbeygale May (Tippy), then aged eleven, sitting on my peg. A bird fell about a hundred yards behind the line, immediately regained its feet, and set off for the wood. Knowing there was no picker-up there, I gave Tippy the nod and off she went, while I concentrated on the last few moments of the drive. When the drive was over a fellow Gun wandered up. 'I'm afraid your dog's got away,' he said, gesturing into the middle distance, where a small black shape could be seen. Crossing my fingers, I replied: 'She's just out on a retrieve, actually.' And sure enough, Tippy hadn't let me down. As she got closer we could see the runner in her mouth, which was duly delivered. A purist would argue that we had broken all sorts of gundog handling rules – working her while I was still shooting, to name only the worst! But that's the joy of having formed a long-term partnership with your fully and painstakingly trained spaniel. Those moments of controlled flamboyance and brilliance in the dog are what make dog training worthwhile. People who don't bother to train their dogs properly ultimately miss out on all that.

This last phase of producing your polished all-round spaniel is crucial, so don't rush it. When training for peg steadiness, begin by volunteering to help out the keeper, especially with jobs like flanking and waving a flag on partridge days. Be happy to be the one walking or acting as back-stop or tapper. All these tasks give you the opportunity to teach your dog to sit and walk patiently to heel while there is a lot of excitement going on. If you have a chance to go pigeon shooting or duck flighting, take your dog and sit him up in the hide with you. Although classed as rough shooting, this makes similar demands of patience and steadiness to what your dog will encounter when you have him on your peg, but without the more formal surroundings of a driven shoot.

When you start taking the dog on driven shoots you have to put him first and sacrifice your own shooting to an extent. To begin with you and your dog should go to the shoot and do nothing. If you can stand on a friend's peg, then you can keep an eye on your dog while he is being shot over, which is hard if you are shooting in the middle of a busy drive. The next stage is to get a friend to share your gun for the day. On the drives when you are not shooting, stand beside your friend with the dog sat up in front of you, facing you, and off the slip. Keep eye contact with your dog for most of the drive so that he knows he shouldn't be doing anything but sitting still. If he makes a move on a fallen

167

As you introduce the dog to peg work put the slip on and leave the lead trailing so that you can step on it if needed (NICK RIDLEY)

bird, check him quietly with your voice and sit him back up again. That's all, no retrieves. At the end of the drive make a fuss of him, put him back on the slip and leave him in the vehicle while you shoot. If you can't get back to the vehicles, give the dog to your co-Gun and get him to stand a way behind the line with the dog on the slip-lead. Your co-Gun should be happy to oblige – after all he is getting a complementary half-day's shooting.

If all goes well, when your final turn to shoot comes, bring the dog with you and sit him up as before, but keep the slip-lead on and let it lie on the ground. Knowing that you are distracted, your dog may very well make a move on the first bird that falls. This is where your co-Gun steps in, or rather on the lead, and brings the dog up short while you give him a verbal rebuke. Enjoy the rest of the drive, but don't do any more driven shooting with the dog on your peg until he has had some more steadiness work. You can volunteer to load for someone or to help the pickers-up next time, so that you can have the dog in a shooting situation without you actually shooting over him.

Once your dog has become steadier and more experienced on the peg, you will want to let him have the reward of an occasional retrieve – just one or two per drive. This is where problems multiply, as pickers-up are notorious for letting their dogs work round the peg, the prerogative of the Gun and his dog. So you have to be a bit territorial and assertive. When you arrive on your peg, take off your dog's slip and sit him up. Look for the picker-up assigned to you. Leaving the dog sat on the peg, walk over to that picker-up and introduce yourself. This is a great start because it shows the picker-up how steady and well-trained your dog is. With the picker-up wrong-footed, tell him that you are training a young dog and would appreciate a couple of dead birds being left. It's then up to you to make sure all your birds are cleanly killed. If the picker-up doesn't oblige, don't make a fuss, just leave the dog in the vehicle for the remaining drives, because there is nothing that will get a young dog running in more than having dead birds retrieved from his nose.

Do be prepared to put the lead on or even pop the dog back in the vehicle if it all starts going pear-shaped. Don't shoot lots of birds over a potential peg dog while he is still inexperienced. Don't let him have too many retrieves and especially avoid runners and strong cock birds at first as they will rev him up. Even if all this groundwork goes well, it is still possible to ruin a dog, even a professionally trained one, if you overstretch him on his first few full driven days on the peg. Although he may be coping with peg work at eighteen months old, remember that he still won't mature fully as a peg dog until he is two-and-a-half or three years old. That first year is vital, so don't overdo it. Even if very little things start going wrong, like the dog being a bit restless, don't ignore it. You must do something about it immediately. Reprimand him, and do some revision before you take him out shooting on your peg again.

There is a great temptation when you have completed training your spaniel, or if you have just got him back from a professional trainer, to go out shooting and show off by sending your dog for everything. It is the worst thing that you can do. Keep your dog well covered-up, away from big temptations and big occasions for at least your first season driven shooting over him. Stick to smaller days of not more than two hundred and fifty birds or so, and even then don't let him do a great deal. Boring as it is, only a few retrieves during the entire day is plenty.

Don't let the dog have too many retrieves (CHARLES SAINSBURY-PLAICE)

At this stage you should also be very selective about which retrieves you do send your dog for. Avoid anything longer than about fifty metres, as it is all too easy for the elastic to snap in these early experiences of work in the field. But don't let him hoover up loads of easy dead retrieves round the peg either. If there are several dead birds lying in plain view, leave your dog sat up on the peg and quickly go and pick all but one or two yourself. Return to your peg and then send your dog for the remaining birds. Make sure he picks the one you want first and then brings it straight back to you without switching to another bird. Inexperienced handlers often find this problem, and complain: 'My dog goes around picking up first one bird and then dropping it for another.' There is no tactful way to put this, but it is the handler's fault, not the dog's. If there are enough dead birds lying around in the open for the dog to be able to run from one to another, then he shouldn't be working at all. That's not what the dog is for and it's not teaching him anything. Go and pick the birds up yourself and if you want him to have a retrieve to reward him, then just leave one behind for him.

Frustratingly, there is really very little retrieving work for a peg dog to do. Even as he gets older and more experienced, the chances are that your dog won't be able to make many spectacular long retrieves off the peg, because the pickers-up have already dealt with those by the end of the drive. Once you have tried handling your dog in the middle of a big shoot with other Guns wandering about across the line, pickers-up and beaters' dogs running around everywhere, and the shoot captain keen to pack up and get to the next drive, you know it's not the time to be playing at field trials. Hard as it is to accept, on those big driven days, it's best to leave your dog at home or in the vehicle, at least until he is an older, semi-retired chap who will be happy just being your mate. I'm lucky to be in the position where I can have my old-timers on the peg with me, occasionally re-enacting their former glories, while the youngsters go rough shooting or compete.

By the time he is into his second season, you will begin to see the dividends of all your training. As he becomes more experienced in all the different areas of spaniel work, your dog will begin to emerge as a fully trained all-rounder. For my dogs which have retired from trialling, the whole season sees them

A water retrieve by a Sussex Spaniel (SUSSEX SPANIEL ASSOCIATION)

171

When working on a driven day pip your dog straight back to you with a retrieve so he isn't distracted by other fallen birds (Nick Ridley)

performing in many different ways. In the late summer I am usually rough shooting over them, particularly on rabbits in the north or in Scotland. They will also be putting a little revision in on their steadiness by dogging-in released pheasant. On the 12th my husband and I go grouse shooting over pointers, where my spaniels take on the role of retrieving, and occasionally flushing, while the pointers do the demanding work of finding the coveys. When we go duck flighting in the autumn, I leave the dogs in the back of the vehicle until we have finished. Then they all get some good work on blind retrieves picking up the duck. Once the driven shooting is in full swing they come and sit on my peg –

the only proviso being that I can only have one on my peg at a time. The old competitive spirit never leaves them, and the idea that a kennel-mate might get to a retrieve first leads to a distinct tendency to unsteadiness. On our own shoot I also work the dogs as sweepers, ranging far and wide searching for runners that have slipped through the net. As the season nears its end, the dogs come into their own rough shooting again, this time as we walk up the woods for strayed pheasant, woodcock and rabbits.

For half the year, the spaniels are kept busy in all these different roles. Their main forte is hunting – whether for game to shoot, or searching for lost wounded game – and their ability at this continues to grow with experience. Inevitably the dogs slow down a little as they get older, but they compensate by becoming very game-wise. It is the same with retrieving, the other major aspect of their work. Even after their trialling days are over, their knowledge of scent enables them to make spectacular retrieves. They have a huge amount of experience, and freed from the constraints of trialling, it is fascinating to watch them work more independently. With spaniels, Cockers especially, steadiness is always going to be the hardest part of the equation, particularly when they are still revved-up from trialling. It takes a lot of concentration on my part to keep them straight. But as they get a bit older, they do get steadier – to the point where they are relaxed on the peg. Tippy loves driven grouse shooting. As soon as we arrive in our butt, she makes herself a little nest (incorporating any cast-off clothing, gun slip, cartridge bag etc that she finds) and snoozes there very happily until the drive is over and there is work to be done!

While you are training your young dog to all these different skills, keep in mind this picture of the end result you are aiming for, but also be aware of how much you are demanding from the dog. He has to adapt to all these different situations, and react accordingly. While an experienced old timer can handle all this on his own, it helps if you can take the pressure off your young dog by doing some of his thinking for him. Many amateurs are quite passive with their dogs, tending to let them do their own thing once training is complete. This is fine with a dog that has been everywhere and done everything, but when the dog is young and inexperienced he needs strong leadership from you. A professional handler can often make a dog look much better than he is by thinking through a situation in advance and giving the dog guidance when needed. So think ahead, maintain your concentration, be alert, patient and consistent. Always have a clearly formed view of what it is you are doing today, and handle the dog accordingly. This is really important with an all-rounder when you will be doing so many different things from one day to the next.

As you pick up your gun in the morning, take a moment to think about the day ahead. Are you a Gun on a driven shoot? The spaniel will need to be in peg-dog mode – everything very disciplined, lots of sitting still and almost no retrieves. Or are you going rough shooting with your friends? Your spaniel will need to be raring to go, full of energy to hunt up game. You will have to be on your toes too, ready to step in at the first sign of unsteadiness. Perhaps you are not shooting at all today, but picking-up. Your youngster will have to use his brain a lot, working on long, difficult retrieves. Remember he needs your direction, and he should be concentrating on you just as much as on the retrieve. Your all-rounder spaniel is always on duty in the field – but as his handler, so are you! Put as much into it as your dog does, and you will have a great day, whatever you are doing.

TROUBLE SHOOTING

My youngster isn't bad on the peg, but as soon as another dog starts retrieving he tries to run in

Pickers-up are surprisingly thoughtless about this. Few pickers-up have ever tried to train a peg dog, or they wouldn't let their dogs make retrieves under the peg dog's nose. I fear there is also an element of human competition in this. I have long since learnt not to mention if I am working a champion, as this leads to a cut throat battle to beat the poor FTCh to every retrieve or flush on the shoot! Speak politely but straightforwardly to the picker-up and explain that you are trying to train a peg dog. It may help, but if not there is little option but to choose a more helpful shoot next time you work your youngster.

I find when I am shooting and working the dog I always seem to be running out of time

Be aware that shoots are not there to provide dog handling opportunities. Trying to be a Gun and pick-up on a big shoot doesn't really work. Instead get together with a few friends and buy a small day on which you can have some shooting, but make dog training and work the primary objective.

My dog has started to be very restless in the hide with me when duck flighting

This can happen if you are using a large calibre and heavy load in a quite en-closed hide. Your earplugs are protecting you from a pretty large bang being made by your gun, which can make even the bravest dog a little gun-shy. Leave him in the vehicle until you have finished, and then enjoy some blind retrieves.

Everybody on my shoot uses a screw, should I get one?
Clearly nobody on your shoot except you is a proper gundog handler. A properly trained peg dog will never need to be tied to a screw. And tying an improperly trained dog to a screw just makes them even madder! If your dog shows any sign of moving, work through the exercises in this chapter and you should soon solve the problem.

Field trialling is well worth trying (CHARLES SAINSBURY-PLAICE)

13.
FACING UP TO A FIELD TRIAL

I f all has been going well with your training, and your first season in the field is flying along, you could well find yourself getting compliments on your dog's work. The icing on this particular cake is field trialling. Now is the time to think about such higher education level work. Whether you actually decide to enter a trial, or would rather just go along and find out a bit more, field trialling will add a new dimension to your dog work. The top gundog trainers, professional and amateur, all agree that a field trial is the acid test. At a trial, the results of your training methods are there for all to see. Success speaks for itself, and if you are looking for a good handler either for lessons, or dog training, or to buy a dog, it is the handler's record in trials which will give you a true picture of his abilities.

But there is far more to gundog trialling than just the handful of leading trainers, and anybody whose dog is good enough has the chance to compete and win on equal terms. However, for a newcomer who wants to find out whether his dog is really as good as he thinks he is, it can be hard to know where to start. This best thing to do is get friendly with someone who is already trialling. Ask gamekeepers and pickers-up, or look at field trial results in the shooting press to find out who to contact. It is also a good idea to get the name of a successful professional and take yourself and your dog to him for a couple of lessons. The professional will be honest about your dog's chances and if he thinks there is potential you will get plenty of help and advice. It's a great opportunity to get connected into the trialling network.

Most trials are run by gundog training clubs which give their members preference in the draw for runs, so you will need to join some clubs. The Kennel Club (See Appendix III) keeps a contact list of all the gundog clubs. If you get keen, be prepared to join many clubs, but remember to make sure they are clubs which do hold Springer and Cocker trials. Some clubs concentrate only on retrievers, and there isn't much point in joining a retriever training club specialising in dummy work when you have a Springer Spaniel who is a brilliant game finder!

Before you enter a trial, do your homework. Go and watch a couple; not only will you see what the form is, but you will also get a better idea of whether your dog is of the required standard. A spaniel trial takes the form of a highly organised rough shooting day. There are six to eight Guns, who walk line abreast through the cover. The line is split in two halves, known as beats, each with three or four Guns covering the section. Two dogs are worked at a time, one on each beat. There are usually two judges (four at the more important trials), who cover a beat each. The trial is usually for sixteen dogs to compete, but sometimes more, especially at the annual championships. The dogs take their turn in pairs, and will have two runs, one under each judge. The competitors whose dogs are waiting for their turn to run walk in a group behind the line, together with the spectators. On spaniel trials it can be very hard to see what is going on, so to get nearer the action you can volunteer to be a game carrier. You can learn a lot from watching the best handlers closely. You might be surprised at how quiet they are, leaving the dog to work with as little interference as possible.

Apart from training, one thing you have to do well in advance is find out what kind of ground the trial is going to be held on. Is it steep, rough, hilly ground so you and your dog need to be really fit? Is it going to be on an estate notorious for birds hiding in massive bramble thickets? Or is it a moorland shoot where the game will be mainly rabbits sitting in rushes and long grass? You will have a much better chance if the trial is suited to your dog's particular likes and dislikes. Some dogs can't stand nettles, so there is no point entering a trial on a low-ground shoot in the early autumn where there are going to be a lot still standing. Remember that most trials held in the summer and early autumn will be on rabbits, a different proposition from pheasants. Never use a trial as a substitute for training. It should be the opposite – get to know your dog's strengths during training and then enter a trial that will suit him. If he has a flashy hunting style, find out which trials have nice open ground and white grass to show him off. A big, powerful dog that is perhaps a bit slower and less athletic but enters thick cover without hesitation would look good on a woodland shoot with a lot of rough cover and brambles. If your dog is not so fit, or perhaps you aren't, stick to trials where the walking isn't so hard. I have seen some potentially good dogs miss out because their handlers can't keep up on tough terrain. A

Keep your dog at the back when competing so that he doesn't get over-excited
(CHARLES SAINSBURY-PLAICE)

bit of homework when you are filling in your entry forms goes a long way later on.

The running order in a trial is decided by a draw a few days before the competition, and you have to make the best of what you draw, even if running late doesn't suit your fizzy dog, or running early isn't so good for your quieter dog. One of the biggest differences between a trial and shooting or training is that there is a lot of waiting around before and after your turn. With only two dogs working at a time, and around sixteen competing, you will spend much of the day walking with your dog on a lead behind the action. For a dog this is as much of a test as the run. If he is a laid-back sort who can handle the excitement,

Double championship winner Simon Tyers with a successful woodcock retrieve
(CHARLES SAINSBURY-PLAICE)

you can walk him along at the front. This can work wonders for the type of dog who needs geeing up. Try to give him some glimpses of the dogs working in front of him and getting retrieves, so he has really got the message when his turn comes. However it is probably more likely that you have a lunatic type of dog, especially if you like Cockers! With these, you need to keep them as far away from the action as possible when you are not on your run. Go to the back of the following group and find people to chat with to make it seem like a normal shooting day. If a bird happens to fall near your dog while it is on the lead walk away so he doesn't get frustrated seeing another dog take a retrieve in front of him.

On the day you shouldn't try to do anything different from when you are going training. You will be nervous when you leave, and it will often be very early in the morning, so don't leave preparations to the last minute. Make sure you have a mobile number of the organiser or one of the other competitors, in case you need to make contact. Know how to get to the meet (use the sat-nav or get directions) and allow plenty of time for your journey. The organiser won't wait for late-comers and it is surprisingly easy to get lost once you are off the beaten track. I'm always getting caught out when I trial in Scotland, where distances are a lot further than they seem. Always keep a spare slip-lead and whistle in the vehicle. Keep all of your paperwork (running order and so on) in a plastic wallet so it doesn't go missing. Don't rely on being able to fill up with fuel during your journey. It is likely that you will be on the road long before rural filling stations have opened. Always carry water with you for your dog; it is important for the dog to be well-hydrated not only to perform physically but to maintain his scenting ability. So pack your bag with water, a drinking bowl, a dog coat if you use one, and a pair of waterproof leggings for you. Put it in the vehicle the night before. And don't forget the dog – it's been known!

People like to think that the top handlers in trialling have a lot of tricks of the trade and gamesmanship to keep them winning. In reality it is like any other performance sport – dedicated training is the only secret. When someone commented to Gary Player that he had had a lucky round of golf one day, he replied: 'Yes, I find the harder I practise, the luckier I get'. It's the same with trialling, you can't have an 'it'll be all right on the night' mentality about gundog competitions. If you have cut corners in training it will show up in trials and things will go wrong. In novice trials you get to see all kinds of carry-on especially with Cockers! There will be dogs pulling on ahead so they are hunting and flushing way out of range of the Guns. Running in to the flush or the shot is another common fault. You even come across dogs that aren't fully on the whistle, leading to frantic peeping by the handler.

The author at the 2009 Cocker Spaniel Championship at Shadwell Estate
(CHARLES SAINSBURY-PLAICE)

Ian Openshaw competing in the 2009 Cocker Spaniel Championships
(CHARLES SAINSBURY-PLAICE)

When everybody moves off from the meet and the trial begins we all get a few nerves. Try to think of it as just another training day. But even the top handlers tend to blow the whistle more than usual when running in a trial. You try to keep it the same as ever, but it is inevitable. For one thing, in a trial situation where there is often a lot of hanging around and distraction, steadiness is important. You always want to be on the safe side and know that the dog is on the whistle. Ian Openshaw – who is probably the most successful trialler of his generation, advises: 'When I go forward and the judge asks me to start my run I have a habit of pipping the turn whistle very quickly after I have first cast the dog out. I let him go only about five metres instead of the normal ten or fifteen metres, and then just pip him in to pass back in front of me. I'm just checking the brakes really.'

183

If your training has been 100 per cent you shouldn't be too nervous when your turn comes to step forward and shake hands with the judge before starting your run. Hopefully you will be looking forward to getting stuck into the cover and showing what your dog can do. Remember also that the judge wants to see a dog doing well just as much as you want your dog to do well. When I began trialling as a complete novice I found the judges really helpful – much more so than in other competitive sports in which I have participated.

As you set out on your run, you need to be very aware of everything: the wind and scent conditions; how the game is behaving; anything that could affect the way the dog works. If you are prepared, you stand a better chance of coping with the situation. Keep your dog working a tight pattern to begin with, so you have control right from the beginning. Letting your dog dash off at the start means you will have a battle to stop him hunting too freely all the way through the run. Keep the dog no more than fifteen metres from you on either side, and closer as it passes in front of you. Another reason for having the dog particularly close at the start of the run is that after the handover from the previous dog, there is an interruption in hunting the cover and it is very easy to have game get up behind you at this moment that wasn't flushed at the end of the previous run.

Try to take your time and don't let your nerves get the better of you. There's a great temptation to go striding off so fast the judge can't keep up with you. Keep making assessments of the hunting conditions. If there is a lot of game around keep your dog as tight as possible so you don't miss anything and have plenty of control if he gets a lot of rapid flushes. If the game is pretty thin, you can relax a little and let your dog take more ground in, but keep him close as he passes in front of you. It's better to go for a safe run even if it doesn't set the world on fire, rather than a fast, stylish one which might end in disaster.

If you spot any nice bits of cover go for them – the judge will tell you if he doesn't want you to go there. Hunt towards where you think there will be a pheasant hiding, but don't miss ground on the way there. Ideally you want to try to find a bird or rabbit as quickly as possible so that you can get it shot and retrieved, which gives you more opportunity to score top marks. If there is a fallen tree, for example, get there quickly because that is where the birds will be. But you also need to be aware that getting into too much game can be a worse problem than too little. Pheasants have a great tendency to run in front of the dog and only flush when they can run no farther, which often means you get dozens of birds all congregating at the end of a long blank piece of cover.

184   That is where experience comes in, because you are going to encounter

Peter Jones competing in the 2009 Cocker Spaniel Championships
(CHARLES SAINSBURY-PLAICE)

situations that may be new to you and your dog, and you have to find solutions even though you are under pressure. This happened to me at a trial in Shropshire on a very wet day. The birds had all been running on down a ditch. My turn to run coincided with the end of the ditch, which was packed with wet pheasants. Tippy (FTCh Abbeygale May) found herself confronted with a number of birds that had nowhere to go. When they didn't fly, she 'retrieved' one – all right, pegged it – and we were put out of the trial. You need to be prepared for such pitfalls and be ready to take preventative action. In this case I should have kept Tippy really close and hunted her in a different bit of cover, away from all the trouble lurking in the ditch. I might not have got a find, but at least I wouldn't have been put out. Ultimately the only way you will learn these things is from your early mistakes!

Another aspect inexperienced handlers often find difficult is working with the Guns. At home we all tend to shoot over our dogs alone or with friends, whereas on trials it is usually a stranger shooting. Don't be intimated. Sometimes a Gun will walk too fast, which can pull the dog forward and result in missed game. If there is only the odd pheasant you might chance missing a bird and let the dog go with the Gun a little bit. But if there is a lot of game about, ignore the Guns and take your time. Occasionally they might walk between you and the dog or walk into cover before the dog has got there. Politely ask them to slow down or even get the judge to ask them. Sometimes the Guns are not very experienced either! So keep your dog as close as possible. This means the flushes are closer, making for easier shooting. With gamekeepers shooting, as you often get, you don't have to worry.

When your dog is flushing the bird, watch it to make sure it is steady, but remember to keep an eye on the bird so you can mark the fall. Most handlers pip the stop whistle, just to be on the safe side. Concentrate on your marking – use a tree or something distinctive that won't move for a mark. Once you are sure of your mark, keep your eye on your dog. Now it's time for the retrieve. The judge will give you his mark and say: 'Send your dog.' Quite often the judge's mark won't be the same as yours! But remember, the judge is always right, at least to begin with. So send your dog to the judge's mark first. You must demonstrate that you can put the dog on where the judge thinks the fall is. If the dog doesn't find there, then by all means you can handle it to where you think the bird is, and hopefully you will have got it right. Most birds don't actually fall that far away so the retrieve should be quick.

The judge will check the bird to make sure your dog has not been hard-mouthed. If everything has gone smoothly he will probably decide that you can proceed to take your second run for the other judge when your turn comes. If your dog doesn't find the bird, the dog from the other beat and his handler will be brought over to try. If they find it, unfortunately that means you will be put out of the trial by an 'eye-wipe'. When neither you nor the other side find the bird, the judges will walk forward to see if they can find it by human searching. Sometimes they do manage to find it. Often this happens if the bird is 'scent-blind' – if it is lying in water or similar. In this case both dogs are out of the trial. So it is a nail-biting time for all concerned! Other faults that will put you out include: missing game; making a noise; unsteadiness; pulling too far in front; and hard mouth. Trialling has a tradition of good sportsmanship. If you're unlucky enough not to complete your first run, it isn't good form to stomp back to your car and head home. Stay on as a spectator and you will gain experience as well as friends in the trialling world. At the end remember to thank your host, the gamekeeper, the organisers and the judges.

Even if you don't want to compete in a field trial with your dog, don't ignore trialling, or believe people who will try to tell you it is all artificial rubbish. I've probably learnt more from just watching trials I have been put out of, than any amount of work in the field. Even if I don't have a dog running, I always spectate at both the Springer and Cocker annual national championships. The first thing I always notice is the most obvious – and it must be said, unflattering – difference between a trial and everyday walked-up shooting over dogs, is that trialling is extremely efficient. The spaniels competing are steady to flush, shot, and fall of game, work within range of the guns and remain under control. They hunt every bit of cover thoroughly so almost no game is missed. All of which means that game, ground game included, is safe and shootable, and is retrieved with a minimum of fuss. How different from the average rough-shooting day, with birds flushing out of range, dogs chasing and retrieves being lost!

But the real point to take away from watching a field trial is that you can achieve this high standard of work at home with your own spaniels and your shooting friends. Most of the dogs we all train and work are bred on almost identical lines to those winning trials, so there's no reason why the dogs themselves shouldn't be capable of it. And if you are conscientious with your training you are halfway there. But the big difference in performance between a trial and an ordinary walked-up shoot is usually due to better handling. All dog work is really only variation on the four basic commands of 'come', 'sit', 'get on' (hunt) and 'get out' (retrieve). It's what you do with those commands that counts.

At one trial I was watching Roy Ellershaw work his Cocker Fernmoss Flow. They found themselves in plenty of game and scent and things could easily have started getting out of control – with the danger of Flow hunting out of shot range or missing game. Roy didn't panic. Instead of slowing the dog down he made sure he hunted a very flat pattern, passing in right in front of his feet with each sweep of its quartering, but letting him go out wide to either side. Roy was confident that a discreet 'pip, pip' of his whistle would turn the dog if needed. This way control was maintained without compromising the dog's speedy and stylish hunting.

When watching trials it is also very noticeable that the top handlers use all the different methods of communicating with their dogs, not just verbal commands or whistling. Body language, especially the hand, is really effective. I have watched Jon Bailey keep his hand low to encourage his spaniels to get

187

their noses down when hunting. When Simon Tyers has to handle a dog on a blind retrieve they rarely have any difficulty because Simon's hand signals are really visible and very precise. Simon also uses his hands to make sure his dog can still see him when bringing a bird back through thick cover. Of course hand signals can't work unless your dog is actually looking at you, but since field triallers' dogs are invariably fixated on them, this isn't a problem.

In fact there is nothing like trialling for building a close bond between you and your dog. Dutch, Lyn, Tippy, Bisto, Fudge – and hopefully soon Ginger and Pepper – have all been on great trialling adventures with me all over England and Scotland. We have learnt together from our mistakes – something the most successful triallers are quick to do. When things go wrong it is impor-tant to analyse the mistake in your own handling rather than blame the dog. When Dai Ormond failed on a blind retrieve with FTCh Rowston Serana at a recent championship trial, he told me 'It was my fault. The bird turned out not to be where the judges had marked it. The dog knew that and wanted to go where it really was, but I didn't trust him and kept moving him away.' The moral is: unless you are absolutely sure you know where a bird is, don't assume you know better than the dog – nine times out of ten you don't!

The author's FTCh Gournaycourt Morag bringing back an eye-wipe on a woodcock (HANS-ERIK SJOBLOM)

Anticipating problems early and solving them quickly is vital to good dog handling, and a talent shared by all the top handlers. For example if your dog is sent on a retrieve with two semi-runners down flapping around, and lots of other birds flushing on the dog's outrun, you have to recognise immediately that there is a potential for chaos. Under these circumstances, an experienced handler sits his dog up for a moment to let everything calm down before then giving the dog a strong clear command not just to retrieve, but which bird is wanted. To cope with these tough challenges you have to be switched-on and concentrating, rather than wandering along with your head in the clouds. The biggest message I always take home from my field trialling is that if you want to get good with dogs, you must engage with your dogs and what you are doing right from the get-go.

TROUBLE SHOOTING

I have started competing in field trials but find I get very nervous

Many top spaniel handlers (including me!) do still get very nervous trialling. Always give yourself plenty of time on the day of a trial, being late makes you even more flustered. If one of my dogs is competing at a major championship I often ask a friend to handle him for me, otherwise my nerves mean I may not do him justice. It does get easier as you get more experienced; just remember that you are among friends – even the judge wants you to do well!

My dog works really well in training, but he won't listen to me when trialling

This is a very common problem and is known as the dog being 'trials wise'. In other words, he has cottoned-on that you can't chastise him during a trial, so he exploits the opportunity to enjoy himself at your expense. The answer is to create mock trials days with your friends. Do everything exactly as you would in a trial, with the one difference that when your dog goes wrong, you can descend on him and give him the shock of his life. Avoid a dog getting trials wise in the first place by making sure your training is 100 per cent before you enter a trial.

How can I tell if my dog might have a hard mouth?

The judge will always check a retrieve that your dog brings back. You can check at home by turning the bird on its back in the palm of your hand and gently feeling for the ribs. Any sharp points or breaking and flattening of the rib cage means that your dog has been hard-mouthed. To double check you can skin a bird and quite clearly see a broken rib sticking through the meat – no good for roasting! Always make sure your dog picks the bird and brings it straight back without any mouthing; use your whistle to return him quickly.

How long before the trial starts should I get there?
Get to somewhere with a bit of public access land very near the trials ground about an hour beforehand. This means you can take your dog out to relieve himself and have a last minute bit of revision before you enter the trials ground. Kennel Club rules state that training of the dog on the trials ground is not permitted, and you must certainly not be seen chastising the dog. Many trialling folk meet for breakfast and a bit of last minute preparation before the trial – the different breakfast spots are well known within the trialling world!

14.
BUYING OR BREEDING THE NEXT DOG

Two great writers on spaniels, Keith Erlandson and Joe Irving, would both agree with the old saying that 'you always make a mess of your first dog'. Certainly I made every mistake in the book with my first Cocker. But in the end the experience is usually a positive one. He may be mad, bad and dangerous to know, but he's still your dog and you have wonderful times together. So most novice spaniel trainers promise themselves: 'I won't make the same mistakes with the next dog'. There will be a next dog, and more, because very few gundog owners manage to stick at just one dog. I have nine dogs at the moment, with ages varying from ten months to twelve years.

When you are training your first dog you get a lot of advice from other dog handlers or from training books. Some of the advice is best ignored, which is fine, as that is usually what the first timer does anyway. Much of the advice is excellent, but unfortunately the beginner doesn't have the experience to use this advice to advantage. When I began training I felt as if I was in a Catch 22 situation, where you needed some practical knowledge to be able to apply the theory outlined in the training manual – but how could I get that experience in the first place? For me the breakthrough really came with my second dog. I actually showed a bit of common sense and bought an experienced bitch who had already won two open field trials handled by Steve Wanstall, and just needed her water test certificate to become a champion. Lynn (FTCh Kelmscott Whizz) was a marvellous schoolmistress for me. When she died at the grand old age of fifteen, I worked out that she and I had actually been shooting together everywhere from John O'Groats to Land's End. What a lot I had learnt from her along the way!

So when you start thinking about buying or breeding your second dog, don't automatically assume it will be a puppy. By now you should have made many gundog training friends and you'll be in the network to hear what dogs may be available. A top trials dog getting ready to retire from competition is ideal to bring you on as a handler, but they can be hard to find. Dogs from professional handlers, who have put them on the transfer list because they will not quite make the grade in competition, are also wonderful to shoot over and gain more experience in training and handling. I very occasionally sell a dog at eighteen months or two years old because it lacks the drive I am looking for as a competition dog. Invariably the new owner is on the phone after a few weeks to describe his new acquisition as 'the dog of a lifetime'. Don't ignore such opportunities if they come your way.

Even if you are set on having a puppy, you should look to the same sources of supply. Don't blindly buy from adverts or cards in the newsagent's window. Be careful about the internet as well. Many less scrupulous puppy farmers push their pups through this outlet, and it can be very hard to spot who is reputable and who isn't. Instead put the word out on the spaniel training network that you are looking for a well-bred puppy and the phone will soon start ringing.

Whether or not you are planning to compete, always look for a pup with lots of field trial champions in the preceding three generations of his pedigree. It's not a matter of being swanky, it's about making sure there are no faults in the family. Physical problems and behavioural issues like hard mouth and speaking are carried genetically, but have been almost completely eliminated in the modern field trial spaniel. To become a field trial champion a dog must be absolutely 100 per cent sound in his health, his athletic abilities and in his temperament, and these are the animals that have improved both Springer and Cocker breeds hugely over the last fifty years. Looking at Ginger and Pepper's pedigree, I notice you have to go back four generations before the first non-FTCh appears. This is exceptional, but they are proof that working ability is definitely carried genetically. As the two pups approach their first birthday they have sailed through their initial training without finding any of it remotely challenging.

When you go to look at a pup, make sure you see the pedigree. If the pup's tail is docked, check the paperwork is in order. There should be a certificate from the vet who docked the puppy. Do remember to match it up with the Kennel Club registration document for the pup. Make sure all the dates are correct. If the breeder doesn't have the right paperwork, it's a deal breaker. It's not just a matter of whether you would be able to compete (all field trial competitors must be Kennel Club registered), but the Animal Welfare Act 2006 actually made it

Mothers and their daughters: Churchview Firefly (top left) *with her daughter Gournaycourt Lemon* (bottom left) *and FTCh Abbeygale May* (bottom right) *with her daughter FTCh Gournaycourt Morag*

illegal for you to have a docked puppy without the appropriate paperwork. If all this is in order, have a look at the bitch and find out a bit about her. Don't make a great attempt to choose 'the right pup'. They should all be toddling around busily, with tails a blur, rushing up to you, chewing your shoelaces and chasing anything remotely chaseable. Being the smallest in the litter isn't a problem as long as the pup is healthy. My best bitch so far was the runt of the litter, and I only kept her by mistake. There will be one though that grabs you, for whatever indefinable reason, so just let your instinct guide you. Do avoid taking your children when you go to choose a pup. If by any chance you decide not to have one from that litter, the journey back home, pupless, with disappointed children, will be miserable.

193

If everything went very well with training your first dog – as hopefully this book will be helping to ensure – you may be thinking of breeding a litter yourself. Responsible and sensible people will tell you this isn't really a good idea. However, I have bred many litters over the years and it has been a very rewarding experience, if stressful at times. It gives a great sense of continuity to be working mother, daughter and granddaughter together. But do force yourself to be really honest about whether your dog is worth breeding from. If your dog has genuinely proved herself in the field and won the admiration of honest judges, both amateur and professional, then you would be within your rights to breed from her, especially if the other parent is equally good. And there are some more subjective criteria which would justify your breeding a litter. For example, if the parent is truly a much-loved animal, or perhaps the last in her line. Maybe she has some fantastic ancestors back down the generations, or she has a wonderful temperament.

Most importantly of all, are there a lot of people who want the offspring? Don't take it for granted that people who compliment your dog, or even say in passing that they would love one of her pups, will actually make good on that. Expect at least half of those who expressed an interest to back out when you are actually looking to find homes for prospective pups. But if there are genuinely half a dozen people, plus you, who would like one of your dog's pups, then – barring any physical problems – there is no reason why you shouldn't go ahead.

Spaniels have few genetic health problems, but you should be aware of PRA (Progressive Retinal Atrophy) which occasionally appears in Cockers. If you have any doubts, get the dog checked over by your vet before you go any further. If all is well, check the pedigree and get some advice on suitable dogs for the other parent. This is much more straightforward if the dog you want to breed from is a bitch, because you will have many proven field trial champion stud dogs to choose from. Don't get side-tracked by people with 'just the dog for your little bitch': The dog in question may be very nice, but you have no idea what genetic horrors of under-bite or hip dysplasia lie in wait from preceding generations. Instead ask around local trialling clubs or go online (many top professionals now have very informative websites), and choose a field trial champion with around 50 per cent champions in the preceding five generations. The stud fee is usually the price of a puppy, or if your bitch really is good you may be paid the genuine compliment of the dog's owner taking a puppy instead of cash.

For those looking to breed from a dog rather than a bitch, matters are slightly more complicated. Owners of good bitches will be looking for a champion, and you shouldn't mate your dog with anything less than a good bitch. To keep breed standards high you really need to prove your dog by getting him noticed – perhaps in working tests or field trials. Remember also that technically the offspring belong to the bitch's owner unless you make a formal arrangement otherwise. An alternative is to buy a good bitch. If she has an excellent pedigree and no faults then she doesn't need to be a champion, but will still be pricey and hard to come by. Once the mating has been arranged, double-check that you have homes ready for the number of pups you expect. This isn't fail-safe, very often you will have more pups or be let down by people. There are many avenues for spare pups, but one with a great feel-good factor is Hearing Dogs for Deaf People, who are always on the look-out for trainable pups, especially Cockers. Contact them through their website (See Appendix III).

A bitch is ready to mate around the twelfth to fourteenth day of her season, and her behaviour (shameless!) will usually be the best signal. Squeeze her bottom gently and if she stands still with tail hooked to one side, then it is definitely time for her mate to get involved. It is best to be present at the mating. They aren't always straightforward, and there are occasional stories of the wrong dog getting in on the act! Once the dogs have tied successfully you can be pretty sure conception has occurred. Although the bitch herself won't need much extra care during her pregnancy, there are some preparations you can make in advance. It is important to make provision for tail-docking. Under the Animal Welfare Act 2006 tail-docking is legal in England and Wales (not Scotland), but you must be able to show the vet that the puppies are definitely going to be worked. A letter from your shoot; your shotgun certificate; any field trial awards the bitch has won; copies of the parents' working pedigrees – all of these should help convince your vet. But don't leave this until the last minute. By law the puppies should be docked on or about the third day after they are born, which is not the moment to discover your vet is unconvinced about the arguments for docking.

Many novices get concerned that, having been mated successfully, the bitch proceeds to show no sign at all of being pregnant for weeks and weeks. With one particularly fit Cocker of mine, whose putative pups had long ago been earmarked, we weren't 100 per cent sure even four weeks before. You can have your bitch ultra-sounded by the vet, but in the natural world animal pregnancies are not spent with paws up 'eating for six' – no matter what the bitch might try to persuade you. Do keep a note of the successful mating (both of them if there were two) and mark the due date in your diary – remembering to keep that day free! Gestation (pregnancy) is around nine weeks (sixty-three days) for most gundog breeds. Try to relax about it all until about three weeks beforehand.

Expect the pregnancy to start showing about three weeks before the due date of birth. It isn't necessary to give the bitch more food at this stage, but make sure the quality of the food is good. I often start adding a dash of sunflower oil or some tinned mackerel to the food at around this stage. Allow the bitch to have as much exercise as she wants. With spaniels they don't really start slowing down until about ten days or a fortnight before the birth. Cockers can look very comical at this stage, rushing around the place like an animated beer barrel on legs! When the pregnancy starts showing you can prepare the whelping box. You can either build your own or buy a kit from Newdog (See Appendix III). There are excellent disposable whelping boxes which make for good hygiene. The box should be big enough for the bitch to stand up and turn round in. There should be a low entrance at the front, and rails round three sides to stop the puppies getting trapped when the bitch lies against the side of the box. Most bitches are pretty good with their pups and take great care not to squash them – and the puppies are surprisingly good at wriggling out from under!

The week before whelping is due, start getting the bitch used to the box. It sounds a small thing, but oddly enough it can be one of the more challenging elements of the whelping process. Most experts suggest putting the whelping box in a quiet, secluded area and this does make great sense. But spaniel owners, especially Cocker Spaniel owners, know that spaniels are a very gregarious breed. They hate being made to go and lie down somewhere out of the action. This usually leads to them abandoning the whelping box in favour of somewhere that has loads of human traffic. With my bitches that is the space behind the kitchen rubbish bin. So I drag out the rubbish bin a week or so before the big day and manage to fit the whelping box into the space. It's important to be flexible about this, because the bitch almost certainly won't be. Another problem with quiet, secluded spots is that they tend to be pretty uncomfortable and boring places for the waiting human onlookers. Ultimately the bitch will let you know where she wants to have the pups and that's usually the best place to put the whelping box.

The other important thing to do at this stage is to plan how you are going to handle the actual whelping. If you have any reason to think the whelping is going to be traumatic, discuss it with your vet. It's also a good idea to get on the local gundog network and find an experienced acquaintance who can be on the end of the phone if things get a bit fraught on the day (more likely night!).

Nine times out of ten, everything will be fine – but if it is both your and the bitch's first time, it's as well to have back up. In this last week before whelping, even the most hyperactive of spaniel bitches do slow down a bit, so don't force her to exercise. Just enough for her lavatory facilities and to stretch her legs is plenty. Remember also that the pups may come a day early, so do have the bitch settled in her whelping box in plenty of time. My bitches always give birth in the kitchen, so in practice that means they start living in the house about a week beforehand, which everybody enjoys.

When the bitch is starting to go into labour she will be restless and uncomfortable. Clean her underparts with gentle disinfectant and make sure she has access to water – she will be off her food by now. The vast majority of gundog whelpings go absolutely fine, and even those that aren't smooth all the way through usually end up with a happy outcome. But every bitch is different, and can take even experienced dog breeders by surprise, much less first-timers. Straightforward parts of the process, like the bitch eating the placenta (afterbirth), are rarely described in the books and can come as a shock to the less earth-motherish of us. I confess to being briefly worried on seeing my first puppy emerge in its foetal sack, little more than a black, fluidy, membranous blob – and nothing at all like the cute pictures in the book.

In several of my bitches' whelpings the first puppy has popped out very comfortably, but particularly with 'maiden' bitches, things can slow down a bit then. As long as the bitch is comfortable, busy cleaning pup one, be patient. Putting the lights out and leaving the bitch alone for a while often works. Some bitches don't like being watched, so try to get an arrangement where you can see without being seen. If there's still a stalemate after half an hour or so, look at the bitch very carefully. Is there a puppy stuck half out? Is the bitch distressed? Is she doing a lot of unproductive heaving? These are signals to get help. The smaller spaniels, Cockers especially, do sometimes have difficulty delivering their pups. A larger than average pup may be slow to deliver, which leaves the ones queuing behind weaker. Like humans, bitches occasionally have pups in the 'breach' (back to front) position, and this is a problem you are going to need help with. Another difficulty is if the foetal sack bursts too soon. Carefully inspecting the birth passage can often let you see these problems and get help immediately.

Most of the time though, everything will go perfectly smoothly, with pups popping out at regular intervals and the mother cleaning up as she goes. Watch out though, if pups are coming quickly, this is when the bitch can miss one in the general mêlée. Clean it yourself with a piece of kitchen towel and then give

197

it to the bitch and check she incorporates it into the rest of the litter. Pretty soon she should have them all neatly rowed up on her teats. And a bonus is that many bitches do all the cleaning up too, so you would never know any of the messy bits had ever happened! Don't interfere too much at this stage. Plenty of rest for all concerned is what is needed at this point. Make sure the bitch has water and check her temperature is normal, but otherwise leave her alone for the time being. She will probably have a big long sleep at this stage.

If she continues to be restless, drinking a lot of water and perhaps licking herself, these are signs of post-partum infection. The vet can prescribe a course of antibiotics which usually clears this up quickly. Any difficulties in suckling should also be reported to the vet. If you do have to pop the bitch to the vet, don't worry too much about the pups. As long as they are in a warm place – by the AGA or with a hot water bottle – they will be fine for a short while. Bitches don't always get their appetites back immediately, even though they are suckling. Again, don't worry too much. Make sure the bitch is drinking water. Tempt her with scrambled egg or rice pudding or minced chicken. My bitches usually have a scrambled egg and sardine celebration breakfast after whelping. Once she has rested and hopefully had a snack, the bitch will want to go outside to the lavatory, which you can let her do. Don't be too concerned if her movements are a bit upset for a while, and be guided by the bitch about when she wants to go out and come back in. She doesn't need proper exercise for at least a week.

For the first couple of days, try not to be constantly interfering with the bitch or handling the pups. The family are going to have to be patient at this point. Even though your children will be desperate to cuddle the pups, they will have to wait a little while. The bitch needs to settle into her new routine as a mother. The only interruption will come on day three when the pups' tails should be docked. Some vets will agree to do a house call, but others may want you to come to the surgery. This of course, is quite a performance! I have a 4x4 with a decent tailgate, so I get someone to help me put the whole whelping box, complete with pups, into the back! The bitch pops in the back with them for the journey. Then we park by the vet's door, and the pups go in and out one or two at a time. The bitch rarely notices that one or another is missing, and the whole operation usually goes surprisingly smoothly.

For the next three weeks you will get into an enjoyable routine. The puppies will be getting bigger and more 'puppy-like' by the day, and the bitch will be eating plenty. Now that she is suckling, she certainly needs to have as much good quality food as she wants. Even before their eyes open, you will be surprised how mobile the pups are – so do keep counting them from time to

Don't make a great attempt to choose 'the right pup', it's usually too early to tell ...

... but occasionally a precocious 'star' will shine out (NICK RIDLEY)

time to make sure one hasn't got itself stuck behind the fridge! You can begin weaning at between three and four weeks. This is an extremely sticky and messy business. When the bitch is outdoors having a little walk, get a couple of puppy feeding dishes – very shallow – and put some gently warmed rice pudding in. Encourage the pups to find the dishes and if you have chosen the right moment they will start licking the rice pudding. If they don't show much interest, wait another day and try again. Don't try to feed the pups while the bitch is there, she will wolf down their rice pudding in seconds! When the moment is right the pups will start showing an interest in the rice pudding. You can help them by putting some on your finger and letting them lick it off. Gradually they will get the idea and start gumming it to death enthusiastically.

As the pups get better at eating, gradually introduce scrambled eggs, finely minced chicken and eventually commercial puppy food. At the same time, the pups should gradually be suckling less. Most of my bitches have been very motherly, and willing to go on suckling for ages. If yours is the same you will need to see that she spends a little less time with the pups. Let her have longer walks. When she has been away from the pups a while, their appetites will have built up and this is the time to feed them. You can let the bitch back in when the pups have finished their meal. This is a good stage to worm everyone! Even when the bitch has been regularly wormed before mating, somehow or other, the pups often manage to pick up worms from her milk, so worming is essential. If a pup isn't thriving, or has an excessively bloated tummy, or has a poor appetite, or licks itself, these are all signs of worms. You should also watch out for any skin problems, as pups can occasionally pick up small mites which are almost invisible to the naked eye, but cause itching. These are easily treated by the vet.

By about the sixth week, weaning should be complete and the pups will have become much more independent of mum. During the transition period of the next week to ten days I let the bitch sleep with the pups but generally during the day she will be out and about. The bitch often tells you when she has had enough of the pups. She gets irritable with them and wants her own space. By now a good litter of pups will be strong and boisterous, getting under everyone's feet, and looking more and more ready to move on to their new homes. You shouldn't let the pups leave until they are eight weeks old, and I often have mine around until they are ten or twelve weeks old and their new owners have a convenient moment to collect them. This eight to ten week stage in a pup's life is great fun for everyone, if sometimes infuriating! And then it's time to start training – and back to Chapter One of the book!

TROUBLE SHOOTING

This is my first whelping, and I'm worried about what to do if something goes wrong

Few of the dog manuals have a section on how it feels when your prized champion bitch has to be rushed to the vet's not once but twice during whelping. And nobody tells you about the reluctance of modern small animal practices to make house calls. So it is wise to be prepared in case the worst happens. Discuss matters with your vet. Also find an experienced dog-owning friend who will agree to be on the end of the phone if you are worried. Whelpings always seem to happen at night, but most of the time they go smoothly.

My bitch has rejected one of the pups although she is OK with the others

In these circumstances, bitches often know best. I gave the kiss of life to a pup four times, but the bitch rejected it every time. When I looked closely I discovered it had been born with a cleft palate and could never have suckled. Sometimes we just have to accept how nature is.

I can't get my bitch to use the whelping box

Watch her carefully to see where she wants to be, and then put the whelping box there. Line it with some of her own bedding and put familiar stuff in it. This can be removed once she has finally settled in.

Appendix I: Other Spaniel Breeds

B y far the most popular and successful spaniel breeds for working are the English Springer Spaniel and the Cocker Spaniel, but there are several other types of spaniel which you may sometimes see out and about in the shooting field. For field trials and working tests they are generally classified as 'minor breeds' – but that doesn't tell the whole story. Some of the 'minor' breeds are actually so rare as to be endangered, and have been classified by the Kennel Club as 'vulnerable native breeds'. The rare breed spaniels have fascinating histories. Until recently some were only present in the showing world, or spotted occasionally as an oddity out shooting. Nowadays rare minor breeds like the Clumber and the Sussex are being re-discovered as working dogs and are gradually becoming more successful.

Other breeds with 'spaniel' in their name are considered to be part of the retriever group or the hunt/point/retriever (HPR) group. Irish Water Spaniels, for example, are tested along with Labradors and Flat-coats as retrievers. Brittany Spaniels compete in the HPR group. But the people who work these dogs are keen to stress that in fact they are genuine all-round dogs which can perform spaniel-type work as well as pointing and retrieving.

The final class of spaniel to be found working in the field is the cross-bred, with Sprockers (Springer x Cocker) by far the most common. Cross-bred gundogs always used to be frowned on, but as the fashion for them has spread among dog owners generally, there are also more to be found out shooting. The main spaniel crosses are with Labradors and poodles. The results can be mixed though – as you might expect! And they can't be competed in field trials as the Kennel Club does not register them.

It has become the norm for shooting folk to blame the showing world for

202

the deterioration in minor breed spaniels. This doesn't quite tell the whole story. Many of the now rare gundog breeds declined greatly in the field as a result of the two world wars of the 20th century. As shooting got going again, keepers and shoot owners stuck with the breeds that were cheap to buy or breed, and easy to train – obviously Labradors and Springers. Even Cockers went into decline after myxomatosis wiped out their major quarry, the rabbit. But in the showing world a few breeders continued with rare and unusual spaniels, although it was inevitable that they would breed for appearance-based characteristics rather than working ability. Now that shooting folk are re-inventing the minor breeds, they are apt to complain about their exaggerated physiques and lack of athleticism, but these dogs might be completely extinct without the show bench. It is also very heartening to see that most of the breed societies are very supportive of the idea of their breed as a working gundog, and many of them have active working sections.

Now that you have succeeded in training the easier type of spaniel, you may be thinking of trying something a bit different. And the minor breeds are certainly different! Here is a brief guide to the rare or unusual breeds and cross-breds worth thinking about.

Clumber Spaniel

This large thick-set spaniel with long white coat and pale liver markings (known as orange), has a very Edwardian feel about it. Imagine a spaniel as depicted by Sir Edwin Landseer, Queen Victoria's favourite artist who painted *Monarch of the Glen*, and you have an idea of what the Clumber is about. The story is that Clumbers were originally used on the Clumber Park estate in Nottinghamshire to blank in large partridge drives. Their slow, lumbering gait would supposedly have made them ideal for this task.

I suspect though, that Clumbers were always something of an eccentricity in the field, more a style statement than a thorough-going working dog. This is certainly true today. Show breeders got hold of Clumbers in the last century and accentuated all the 'oil painting' features – size, heavy build, over-feathering – with the result that the breed became more or less useless as a working dog and developed health problems as well. Although not endangered, the gene pool for Clumbers is now small, which makes improving the breed even harder.

Recently the heroic efforts of Debbie Zurick and her husband, Jon, have done much to reinstate Clumbers as a working dog – to constant opposition from showing breeders. Debbie only breeds from more athletic Clumbers who

Clumber Spaniels are now making great strides out shooting (NICK RIDLEY)

have been proven in the field and have good hip scores and no health problems. She is gradually developing a strain which will be an enjoyable shooting companion, though Clumbers are never going to set the cover on fire.

Clumbers tend to be quite strong-willed. They have excellent noses, but fail to see the point of hunting cover which does not contain game – always a drawback in the field trialling world, for example. But I can see a future for the Clumber as an all-rounder and stylish ornament on the peg, a role to which it is much better suited than currently trendy Cockers.

- **INFO:** Listed by the Kennel Club as a 'vulnerable native breed'. Debbie Zurick is secretary of the Working Clumber Spaniel Society (See Appendix III).

Field Spaniel

Sadly this beautiful Spaniel is now quite rare. It looks somewhere between a large, athletic Cocker and a mini-sized Flat-coat retriever. It is whole coloured, usually black or red, with plenty of feather and a handsome head. I have only seen a couple of Field Spaniels working, and they occasionally compete at the minor breed spaniel trials and working tests held once or twice a year.

Again this is a dog which the showing people got hold of. However the breed society, The Field Spaniel Society, is keen to continue and promote the breed's credentials as a working dog. Those you occasionally see out shooting still retain their athletic build, but unfortunately their instinctive working ability seems much reduced. Those that I have watched showed poor concentration and a lack of scenting.

However, some gundog trainers believe that a similar job could be done with Field Spaniels as with Clumbers. Field Spaniel handlers tend to be showing people who are novices in training and working gundogs, and it may well be a case of training the trainers. When I hosted a minor breeds field trial I noticed a Field Spaniel showing some drive in its hunting, but it was being stopped all the time by the handler, who confessed she wasn't sure what the dog was meant to be doing when hunting – but she was very enthusiastic about learning! So maybe there is hope for the Field Spaniels, if only something can be done before the gene pool gets even tinier.

- **INFO:** Listed by the Kennel Club as a 'vulnerable native breed'. The Field Spaniel Society is active in encouraging gundog work (See Appendix III).

Despite its name, the Field Spaniel is a rare sight in the shooting field (NICK RIDLEY)

205

Bill Cadwell's Sussex Spaniels work as well as the Cockers they resemble (NICK RIDLEY)

Sussex Spaniel

This is another wonderful old breed of spaniel which is now endangered. The rise in popularity of the Cocker hasn't helped the Sussex, as they are essentially similar breeds. Some of the larger old-fashioned strains of Cocker are often confused with the Sussex. Sussex Spaniels are a little larger and more thick-set than Cockers, and nearly always whole-coloured chocolate (officially: golden-liver).

Some are worked on shoots in the south-east of England, where I have been very impressed to watch them, especially those bred and trained by Bill Cadwell – who is doing so much to ensure the working future of Sussex Spaniels. Like many of the rare breed spaniels, they can be rather stubborn and hard to train, but I think their independent nature makes them rewarding dogs to be with. Those I have watched are slower and less stylish in their hunting than Cockers, but they have great determination. Unlike many of the rare breeds, they seem to have retained their intelligence and innate aptitude for gundog work. An idiosyncrasy of the Sussex is that it is the only breed of gundog allowed to speak (bark) when it has found game. Personally I have always thought it made great sense to have a dog that will let you know when there's a rabbit hiding, another plus for the Sussex!

The bad news is that few working Sussex Spaniels are being bred. An attempt to revitalise the breed would probably mean bringing in new genetic material, possibly from larger-sized strains of working Cocker, but this would be frowned on by the Kennel Club and breed society. Neither the Cocker nor Springer Spaniel is historically a pure bred dog, and where the very rare gundog breeds are concerned it may be that the need to expand the gene pool takes precedence over modern ideas of breed standards.

- **INFO:** Listed by the Kennel Club as a 'vulnerable native breed'. The Sussex Spaniel Association is very active, with Bill Cadwell as field trial secretary. Visit the website or e-mail Bill (See Appendix III).

Welsh Springer Spaniel

There is much confusion in gundog circles between Springer Spaniels from Wales and Welsh Springer Spaniels – two very different things as they say! Lots

Welsh Spaniels are a distinct breed from Welsh-bred Springer Spaniels and have unusual red colouring (NICK RIDLEY)

of top handlers in Wales breed and compete the standard English Springer Spaniel (ESS). But the true Welsh Springer Spaniel is much less well known. It is a little smaller than the average ESS and is very handsome with red markings on a white coat.

The main association responsible for Welsh Springers is the Welsh Springer Spaniel Club, and they are keen to get away from the idea that the Welsh is another of the minor breeds that is basically just a show dog. The society states: 'The Welsh Springer is a dual purpose spaniel, in that the breed has not split into show and working types and we believe that it is important to develop the natural working instincts of the breed whilst breeding from sound stock. We gain pride from the fact that our dogs can be worked seriously one day and be shown seriously the next.'

The few that I have seen working are certainly athletic and very eye-catching on a shoot, but look to me as though they could be quite difficult to train.

- **INFO:** There are several societies including the North of England Welsh Springer Spaniel Club; the South-Eastern Welsh Springer Spaniel Club; and the Welsh Springer Club of South Wales. For an overall introduction, visit the Welsh Springer Spaniel Club's website (See Appendix III).

Irish Water Spaniel (retriever)

If you were competing in a field trial with your Irish Water Spaniel, you would be put in a retriever trial and not be expected to do any hunting. This doesn't thrill the Irish Water Spaniel Club, who insist that the dog is very much an all-rounder, saying: 'it is a multi-purpose gundog with origins as a hunting, retrieving, wildfowling and water dog.'

It is also one of the most impressive and attractive-looking dogs you will come across out shooting. It is roughly the size of a Labrador, but remarkable for its almost poodle-like coat. The breed standard describes: 'dense, tight, crisp ringlets, free from woolliness. Hair having natural oiliness' – but to you and me, it's just a Rastafarian dog with dreadlocks! The coat's colour is a rich dark liver with a hint of burgundy, the dye-job humans pay a fortune for.

If I were ever to move away from Cockers and Springers, the Irish Water Spaniel is the dog that would tempt me. I would like to train it for its original purpose in wildfowling and HPR out on the hill, but so far I have only seen them being used as picking-up dogs.

- **INFO:** Listed by the Kennel Club as a 'vulnerable native breed'. For a full picture of the breed and news of working success, go to the Sporting Irish Water Spaniel Club website (See Appendix III).

Brittany Spaniel (hunt/point/retrieve)

Again, another 'spaniel' that is officially not a spaniel but an HPR dog. In fact the Kennel Club now refers to the breed simply by the name 'Brittany'. But I have still included it here, because it looks very spaniel-like (a bit like a Cocker on very long legs!), and would certainly be interesting for spaniel lovers who want to branch out into the world of pointing – a natural extension of hunting, and tremendous fun.

Brittany Spaniel on point (ANNE R D MASSIE)

In its work the Brittany also shows spaniel-like qualities, being a rapid, flowing hunter. They are very versatile being as much at home in woodland as in open ground and adjust their hunting techniques accordingly. Watching them work in a pointer test, they looked stylish, but quite hot. Steadiness would obviously be really important in training. But Brittany handlers insist they make good picking-up dogs as well as for shooting over.

- **INFO:** The Brittany Club of Great Britain has a very helpful website (See Appendix III).

Cross-breds

The main cross-breds are the Sprocker (Springer x Cocker); the Springador (Springer x Labrador) and the Cockerdoodle or Cockerpoo (Cocker Spaniel x Poodle). Cross-bred dogs are increasingly fashionable throughout the dog world, but have been around for a long time on the shooting field. Those who criticise cross-breds should remember that all spaniels and setters were produced by cross-breeding various different European hunting dogs from the Middle Ages onwards.

Today the aim of a cross-bred is to get a dog with all the virtues and none of the vices of the two original breeds. Unfortunately this ideal outcome is far from guaranteed. But feedback from an article in *The Field* assured me that many different cross-breds are out there successfully working – even the Cockerdoodles! The most successful cross-breds are often second generation that have been bred back in (known as F2 hybrid), so that you end up with an offspring that is two thirds Cocker and one third Springer. This is especially so with the poodle introductions.

- **INFO:** There are no formal breed societies for cross-breds, and they cannot be Kennel Club registered. This is a drawback for buyers as there is little protection against unscrupulous breeders, so look for your cross-bred by word of mouth.

APPENDIX II: GLOSSARY

COMMANDS

Come/repeated pip, pip, pip on whistle/both hands down patting thighs – all these mean 'return' and can be taught from weaning accompanied by the puppy's name

Dead – verbal command used to encourage dog to yield up his retrieve to handler, not really necessary

Fetch – means retrieve. Can be introduced from the time you start rolling tennis balls etc for the young pup which he retrieves instinctively

Get On/hissing between teeth/low, sweeping gesture with hand – this is the command to hunt, and can be introduced as soon as the pup is out and about and begins to hunt instinctively

Get Out/accompanied by hand gesture indicating direction to travel, low if near, high if far or definitely blind – is used for blind retrieves (ones whose fall the youngster has not been able to see). Introduce with blind retrieves

Gone Away – tells the dog that the flushed game has not been shot, so no need to retrieve

Hup/single long blast on whistle/traffic-stopping gesture with upraised hand – all three, voice, whistle and hand, mean 'sit'. Generally spaniels are told to 'hup' rather than sit, but you can use sit if you wish. This is the first and fundamental command, and can be taught from the time the puppy is eating all of his meals out of a feed bowl, that is after weaning is complete

Leave That – tells the dog not to pick up or flush something he has come across, whether it is game (live or dead) or simply undesirable litter. Can be combined with stop whistle

Left/hand outstretched signal – not used as a verbal command, just a hand signal for directions

Right/hand outstretched signal – not used as a verbal command, just a hand signal for directions

Stay – verbal command to ask the pup to continue to sit, but many professionals don't use it as the pup should in any case continue to sit when told until he gets his next command

Turn/short double-pip on whistle – not used as a verbal command, just a whistle command to get the pup to turn and quarter properly when hunting. Also used when giving directions on a blind retrieve

TERMS

Back wind – wind coming from behind the direction in which the dog is hunting

Blind – the dog has not seen where the game has fallen

Bolt – the dog causes a hare or rabbit to run out from its seat

Chasing – the dog chases the game he has flushed (a fault)

Cheek wind – wind coming from the side of the direction in which the dog is hunting

Cover – undergrowth or planted vegetation likely to provide hiding places for game

Drop on command – the dog sits when the stop whistle is blown or he is told hup or he sees the hand signal

Drop to flush – the dog sits and watches the bird fly away or the rabbit bolt

Drop to shot – the dog sits when he hears a gunshot

Dummy – canvas or other object used to simulate game during training

Fall – where shot game hits the ground

Find – the dog discovers game

Flush – the dog causes a bird to take off and fly from its hiding place

Game – any quarry to be shot, e.g. rabbit, pheasant, grouse, hare etc

Ground – the area to be hunted over

Ground game – rabbits or hares

Hand signals – using hands to show a dog what to do

Handler – the person in charge of the dog

Handling – giving a dog commands, especially on a blind retrieve

Hard mouth – the dog grips the game while retrieving it, causing broken ribs (a fault)

Hunt – the dog searches for his quarry; spaniels do this by scent, mainly ground scent

Indoor pen – wire-mesh kennel used for dogs when indoors or in the back of vehicle

Loose game – birds or rabbits shot which the dog has not previously flushed

Mark – the dog sees where the game has fallen

Missing game – the dog hunts over ground containing game without discovering it

Pattern – the overall route taken by the dog when quartering

Pulling – the dog is not quartering properly and tending to run forward towards the game (a fault)

Quarter – the zig-zag hunting technique used by the dog so as not to miss any ground

Rabbit pen – training aid used to teach hunting and steadiness

Running-in – the dog runs to the fallen game and retrieves it before being sent (a fault)

Seat – the hiding place of a rabbit

Slip-lead – rope-loop lead used for gundogs. Do not use in conjunction with collar

Speaking – the dog barks (a fault)

Steadiness – the dog remains obedient to all commands, even in the heat of hunting and flushing

Style – the appearance and behaviour of the dog when hunting (should be thorough, active and athletic)

Vermin – foxes, magpies etc

Whistle – vitally important for giving commands, 210 ½ usually used for spaniels

Wind – carries scent to the dog's nose

Appendix III: Useful Contacts

AirKONG retrieving trainer	www.kongcompany.com kong@kongcompany.com
Brittany Club of Great Britain	www.brittanyclub.co.uk
Cadwell, Bill	William.cadwell@btinternet.com
Cockers-on-line chat room	www.cockersonline.co.uk
Dog Theft Action	www.dogtheftaction.com
Hearing Dogs for Deaf People	www.hearingdogs.org.uk
(The) Kennel Club	www.thekennelclub.org.uk 0870 6066750
Field Spaniel Society	www.fieldspanielsociety.co.uk
French, Paul	www.paulfrenchvideos.co.uk
Lintran	www.lintran-products.co.uk
National Dog Warden Association	www.ndwa.co.uk
Newdog Ltd	www.newdog.co.uk
Petlog scheme (KC)	www.petlog.org.uk
professional trainers	www.dog-n-field.co.uk or www.ukgundogs.org
Sporting Irish Water Spaniel Club	www.siwsc.org.uk
Sussex Spaniel Association	www.sussexspaniels.org.uk
Turner Richards	www.turnerrichards.co.uk
Tyers, Simon	www.hawcroftgundogs.co.uk
Welsh Springer Spaniel Club	www.wssc.org.uk
Working Clumber Spaniel Society	www.workingclumber.co.uk

INDEX

TRAINING NOTES

TRAINING NOTES

TRAINING NOTES